BIG, EASY
STYLE

BIG, EASY STYLE

CREATING ROOMS YOU LOVE TO LIVE IN

BRYAN BATT

WITH KATY DANOS

Photographs by Kerri McCaffety

CLARKSON POTTER/PUBLISHERS

NEW YORK

COVER
Designer Melissa Rufty creates a masterful mix in Sally and Richard Edrington's Garden District cottage.

PREVIOUS PAGE *A pair of Mario Villa chairs that I gave my brother Jay and his wife, Andrée, as a wedding gift were some of the few things salvageable from their home after hurricane Katrina. This one, re-covered in a fabric by Brunschwig and Fils, sits proudly in their new home against the Benjamin Moore wall color Davenport Tan and Kravet silk drapes.*

RIGHT *A silver-leafed branch lamp from Hazelnut lends an organic twist to this gleaming grand hall.*

NEXT PAGE *In one of my creative spurts, I painted this colorful grid of acrylics to hang in my carriage house.*

CLARKSON POTTER is a trademark and POTTER with colophon is a registered trademark of Random House, Inc.

Library of Congress Cataloging-in-Publication Data
Batt, Bryan.
  Big, easy style / Bryan Batt. — 1st ed.
     p.   cm.
  1. Interior decoration.   I. Title.
  NK2115.B325   2011
  747—dc22   2010035564

ISBN 978-0-307-59190-6

Printed in China

Principle photography by Kerri McCaffety; additional photography by Erik Johnson, pages 6, 25 (lower left), 28, and 31; and David Ash, pages 93 (bottom left), 186, 188, and 189

Book design by Stephanie Huntwork
Jacket design by Stephanie Huntwork
Jacket photography by Kerri McCaffety

10 9 8 7 6 5 4 3 2 1

First Edition

FOR MY BEAUTIFUL NIECES,
BAILEY AND KELLY

CONTENTS

INTRODUCTION

SOME MAY ARGUE that having opposable thumbs or a soul is what separates us from the beasts. But I'll always argue that our ability to choose a paint color, artfully accessorize a coffee table, or toss a fabulous pillow is a gift from the gods. And I believe the knack for design and the confidence to feather your nest can be cultivated. Good taste or style is something that's developed with practice and patience, and many times we just need someone or something to point us in the right direction. How we decorate the spaces we live in is an opportunity for us to express our individuality, and when there is synergy between a home's great style and its owner's personal flair, it is nothing short of divine.

So many people, myself included, can be intimidated when faced with an empty room, and rightfully so: the endless possibilities for a space can be daunting. I say forget about pulling together the perfect room and focus instead on the fun. It's time to break a few rules, take a few risks, and explore your passions. The only bad choice is making no choice at all. Don't worry. Mistakes will happen during the process; after all, that's how some of us got here!

As an actor, I like to take the same approach with home design as with playing a complex character, since both are like solving a puzzle: you have to start with an open mind, do your research (it never hurts to learn your lines early), and then begin experimenting. When first cast in a role, I always start by gathering as many clues about the character as possible from the script, historical facts, and life experiences. This helps to create a multilayered character that is emotionally authentic as well as entertaining. Similarly, with interior design, the same rules apply. Collect information about the home's "cast of characters," study the architectural elements at play, and then embark on the rewarding journey of creating functional and nurturing environments. Whether in acting or designing, attention to detail is essential to producing a well-rounded character or an aesthetically exciting room. As any good actor knows, developing a role is ongoing and ever-evolving, which is a good philosophy to apply to every aspect of your life and home. You should never feel like the process is finished—honestly, no actor ever wants the final curtain to fall.

I have been mad for design for as long as I can remember, and my hometown of New Orleans played a large part in shaping my aesthetic as well as my approach to décor. As a young boy I played in a picture-perfect midcentury modern home nestled

OPPOSITE *Only an act of God could keep me from antiquing at Karla Katz's smashing shop on Magazine Street.*

in the Lake Vista neighborhood of the city, while my grandmother lived in a columned Greek revival home on St. Charles Avenue. Various family members and friends lived in myriad architecturally diverse homes characteristic of the city. From opulent Garden District mansions to small pied-à-terre apartments in the French Quarter, I was exposed to many different styles of design and décor. I loved every bit of it and would even replicate the various styles in my childhood tree house. Some of my early attempts at drapery did not hold up under the oaks and humidity, but my tin can sconces were killer.

My mother and I were regulars at the antiques shops throughout the Big Easy, and when my parents built their dream home, I gladly accompanied them to design meetings and buying trips to furniture markets. With this exposure, I fell in love with different periods and styles of design, which I have always accepted as a good thing.

When acting on Broadway, I find myself drawn to the design district; the Decoration & Design Building; and the humongous gift, furniture, and antique shows all over New York City for an alternative artistic outlet. When I lived in a one-bedroom apartment on the Upper East Side, my closets were always crammed with luxurious fabrics, while two storage units held everything else I was collecting for my nonexistent pie-in-the-sky country house. Over the years, when not trodding the boards of Broadway,

I would assist friends and family in decorating their apartments and homes.

For years my partner, Tom Cianfichi, and I dreamed of opening our own home furnishings and fine gift shop in New Orleans. On each of our many trips back home from New York, we would devote at least one day to explore Magazine Street, one of the most charming and stylish shopping boulevards in the country, which is where we decided to open our shop. We named our store Hazelnut in honor of my grandmother Hazel Nuss (who was also a bit of a nut). Armed with my stacks of sketchpads and Tom's retail expertise, we opened our doors in 2003. Little did we know that our country house would not be a two-and-a-half-hour drive upstate from Manhattan but rather a two-and-a-half-hour flight down yonder.

We brought to the Big Easy our own take on cosmopolitan style, and if we didn't find exactly what we wanted in the market, we designed it. Almost instantly, our little boutique became a beloved destination spot for both in-the-know locals and visitors alike. Hazelnut is filled with colorful, classic, and distinctive furnishings and decorative accessories, treasures that I find bewitching. I am always overjoyed when customers feel the same way—there is nothing quite like a standing ovation.

My creative spirit is deeply rooted in the exuberance of New Orleans, which has a soul like no other city in America. Our

courageous people celebrate the unique architecture, music, cuisine, and history on a daily basis and the artistic parade is constant. There is a beloved phrase here, *laissez les bons temps rouler,* which means "let the good times roll," a philosophy that works in both life and design. Years of performing on stage and on screen, immersed in dazzling costumes, on breathtaking sets, and under fabulous lighting have done nothing to dampen my belief that your surroundings must entertain you while allowing your imagination to take center stage.

I hope that the following chapters will encourage your inner designer as I present what I love about stylish, easygoing spaces. The homes that grace these pages exemplify the beauty and true personal style of each home owner and the talents of the designer.

It's easy to create spaces like these in your own home. Just keep in mind the following dogmas that have never failed me: If it looks right, it is right; and if it don't fit, don't force it. Beyond that, it's your home, your adventure! Remember, just like in life, it's not where you start, and it's not where you finish, but it's the thrill of the journey that counts. Enjoy the ride!

ABOVE *Tom and me in our Magazine Street shop.*

1
DON'T BE AFRAID OF COLOR

Honestly, what did color ever do to you? I have never bought into the idea that we need to be afraid of color, play it safe, or tiptoe around it. Such an easy design element is not something to avoid but rather embrace wholeheartedly. After all, it can only calm, stimulate, or energize with its countless hues. It is the surest and most cost-effective way to change the entire mood of a room and create drama in your home—so bring on the color in all its glory.

COLOR YOUR WORLD

COLOR TIP Saturated colors can be used on your furnishings and accessories rather than on the walls or ceilings if you prefer. A neutral wall will sometimes beg for you to hit it with a splash of color to make the eyeballs pop.

OVERLEAF *A painting by harouni paired with a burgundy wall color is a striking study in red.*

ABOVE AND RIGHT *Benjamin Moore's Bittersweet Chocolate walls and a lipstick-pink settee are a delicious combination. New Orleans Toile drapes are a sophisticated backdrop for the shot of hot pink velvet.*

Use color with confidence as you establish the overall scheme for each room. Even before you purchase your very first stick of furniture or settle on a specific design, you can go a long way toward focusing your ideas just by nailing down the colors that you love and want to live with every day. Choosing a paint color can feel like a big decision, because it will greatly dictate the mood and impact of the room. But don't let that immobilize your decision making. Many people are so concerned about choosing the wrong color that they yield to indecision and end up with something blasé. Try hard to persevere—making this mistake only denies your true passions and will leave you feeling dissatisfied in the end.

Remember that your eye and your gut will never lead you astray. Sometimes you may be forced to rethink shades or intensity, but I say, like peace, give color a chance. By that I mean all color, not only the richly saturated and vibrant tones, but also the palest of pales and iciest tints. I am an equal opportunity rainbow employer. If you like beige, use it with gusto—I adore the classic elegance of the perfect shade of fawn or flax—but by all means, don't choose a neutral just to play it safe. You'll only be sorry, not to mention quickly bored. And boredom I don't do.

Know what colors you truly like and dislike; it'll make your job much easier. No matter how bold, you will *never* tire of a color that you love. You will only want more of it. And remember it is only a can of paint—the color can always be changed. If you are still feeling timid but are craving a color fix, try your idea out on a pillow or an accent piece before going hog wild. But whatever you do, don't be too cool for color. It can be your very best decorating secret. And once you get started, don't stop till you get enough.

IN LIVING COLOR

I love to see an entire room lacquered in one fabulous color, enveloping the senses like a cocoon. A room with a strong color identity has the power to impact your emotions and lift your spirits. But every color triggers an emotional response, so don't think only of vibrant, saturated colors; the softest of hues are just as effective in setting an evocative mood as the bold ones. (If you really want someone's attention, try whispering; if that doesn't work, then sing out loud.) I love to slather on color, often choosing to paint the molding and trim in the same shade, with just a change in finishes, such as from matte to high gloss, to highlight details. This modern approach further amplifies the dramatic effect of your color choice.

OPPOSITE *Etro's Haori fabric introduces all the exuberant colors at play in this family room, which is lacquered in Benjamin Moore's Cote of Arms peacock blue.*

ABOVE *There is no denying the powerful energy and drama that a fiery crimson painting by James Beamon from Cole Pratt Gallery immediately brings to this colorful décor. Turquoise cowhide-covered accent chairs are a flawless accent.*

GET A COLOR CLUE

To help you envision what direction to take your color "imagination," allow yourself the time and space to think about some very basic concepts. The color solutions that feel most appropriate for you will then begin to emerge. The most important thing is how you will want to feel in the room, not how well you adhere to a list of rules.

SIZE DOESN'T MATTER

I don't buy into the rule that size should dictate shade, and I urge you to avoid this trap as well. Yes, lighter colors can be expansive, and layers of whites can reflect light and make a room feel bigger, but even the best of ecrus will never buy you additional square footage. So remain open-minded when selecting what will work best for the actual rooms at hand.

LET THE SUN SHINE IN

When I think about color, light is far and away a greater factor than the size of the room. Ask yourself how much natural light the room gets, from what exposure, and for how many hours. I always start with thinking about the light that enters the room, along with how bright and energetic—or, the flipside, how dark and moody—I want a room to feel. All of these factors help me establish the intensity of color that I'm seeking.

Other Color Considerations

By contemplating these questions, you can veto certain shades from the get-go and move forward with ones that really capture your imagination.

- Is this space a daytime room, like a breakfast room or playroom? Or is this an evening room to relax in, like a living room or library?

- Is this a room where you will spend a great deal of time multitasking, like a kitchen or office? Or is this a room for more intimate use, like a dining room or bedroom?

- Is there a nice view outside that leads you to a particular color family, like lush foliage, rolling hills, or a crystal clear lake?

- Are there architectural problems that require camouflaging, like too many doors in the room, a funky angular ceiling, or a choppy floor plan? (Tip: paint it all one color.)

- Do you have a favorite piece of art, a rug, or a fabric with colors that make you smile or inspire you?

When in doubt, go with your gut!

OPPOSITE *Colors pulled from a silk kimono have a cocooning effect in the bedroom. Benjamin Moore's Sealife for the walls, and blush, pomegranate, and lilac fabrics round the look. It's punctuated by a shiny white porcelain elephant from Hazelnut.*

YOUR COLOR PALETTE DECODED

Once you have an idea of which color to start with, then it's time to entertain the idea of choosing *more* colors of different tones or contrasting hues to pull it all together. Colors can be mixed, chopped, blended, and pureed to various degrees, and just like with cuisine, your personal taste should dictate the outcome. Choosing color combinations and developing a color palette for your home are similar in many ways to building your wardrobe. You begin by using your favorite colors on key items (perhaps the walls, sofas, or drapes), and then you layer in the colors of various accents and accessories (rugs, art, lamps) that will make your main choices pop. This way, the palette can be easily changed and refreshed as your look evolves.

COLOR TIP The ceiling should get as much attention as the walls, treated as another wonderful opportunity to use color to captivate the senses—it should never be an afterthought. Avoid the obvious route of plain-old ceiling white. I often paint the ceiling in the very same color as the walls, perhaps in half the strength, to create a layered, moody effect.

OPPOSITE *Black can be a valuable grounding force in a multicolored room. Found in the artwork by Aaron Collier from Cole Pratt Gallery, lamps from Jon Vaccari Design, and a high contrast fabric from Schumacher, black serves the delightful palette dutifully. And note: a snappy orange chapeau never hurt anyone.*

WORKING THE RUNWAY

I am intrigued by the interesting details and textures of fashion and haute couture and get immediate design gratification from simply strolling through the salons of Oscar de la Renta, Valentino, and Zac Posen. On the flipside, the wonderful color combinations shown on the pages of catalogues such as J.Crew can be inspiring and are delivered right to your doorstep. For years I have gathered tear sheets from my favorite fashion magazines like *Vogue* and *Harper's Bazaar,* and I also collect color and fabric swatches, ribbons, and trims, as well as any bauble, bangle, and bead I can get my paws on. In New York City, I hit the fashion district side streets, especially M & J Trimming, Tinsel Trading Company, and B & J Fabrics. In New Orleans, nothing beats Promenade Fine Fabrics on St. Charles Avenue. I've been visiting Mr. Halpern, the proprietor, since in utero and always stock up on the best couture materials and trimmings. Even one fabulous designer color or print that calls out to you can ignite endless creative possibilities for home décor. Using your fashion sense as a starting point for choosing color is a great idea, because it's really as simple as this: you should only paint or accessorize your home in colors that you look absolutely divine in. It's your home, so look fabulous in it!

PAINT BY NUMBER

I love paint colors, especially their clever and often surprisingly appropriate names, and I never tire of perusing paint chips and studying them in combination with all my favorite fabric swatches. At any given moment, you will see little paint cards taped to my walls as I contemplate my next change of mood or redecoration. I hope this list of my favorites will inspire you to start thinking more about your own favorite hues. Some of these colors are tried and true, and some are more adventuresome. I love them all and would use them again and again, if and when the right opportunity presented itself.

MY FAVORITE WHITES

Super White by Benjamin Moore
Linen White by Benjamin Moore
Ivory Bracelet by Ralph Lauren
Cloud White by Benjamin Moore
White by Benjamin Moore
Petticoat White by Ralph Lauren
Chalk White by Ralph Lauren
Decorators White by Benjamin Moore

MY FAVORITE PINKS

Autumn Red by Benjamin Moore
Venetian Red by Ralph Lauren
Tara by Benjamin Moore
Springtime Bloom by Benjamin Moore
Pink Cherub by Benjamin Moore
Strawberry Sherbet by Benjamin Moore
Hearts Delight by Benjamin Moore
Secret Garden by Benjamin Moore

WHITE Don't be fooled: white *is* a color. It is clean, cooling, and soothing, especially in warm climates. The layering of whites, pearls, and creams can create an inimitable richness and depth that illuminates all in its presence. White also helps create a fresh, natural backdrop for myriad looks, from the timeless combination of blue and white to the Hollywood black and white glamour of a Horst photograph. What I love about an all-white room is that just the teeniest drop of an accent color makes a huge impact.

PINK Pink is not just for girls. There is an inherent beauty and sensuality that shades of pink evoke. The flush of the cheek, the interior of a shell, the bloom of a peony— these images all epitomize warmth and life. Your initial instinct might be to use pink only in bedrooms, but these sophisticated, warm tones look great in all living areas. Shocking pinks, such as the saturated fuchsias found in Indian textiles, can look outstanding in dining rooms, powder rooms, and halls, which are often small spaces screaming for a big identity.

OPPOSITE *In Jay and Andrée Batt's dining room, a layered repetition of moody blues is a dreamy use of one soft, saturated hue. Decorative painter Madilynn Nelson applied five layers of crushed marble and pigment to create venetian plaster walls that mirror the Kravet seaglass damask drapes and painted antique chairs.*

MY FAVORITE REDS

Dressage Red by Ralph Lauren

Stadium Red by Ralph Lauren

Merlot Red by Benjamin Moore

Stop by Sherwin-Williams

Heritage Red by Benjamin Moore

Spring Tulips by Benjamin Moore

Million Dollar Red by Benjamin Moore

Classic Burgundy by Benjamin Moore

MY FAVORITE ORANGES

Orange Parrot by Benjamin Moore

Orange Burst by Benjamin Moore

Copper Harbor by Sherwin-Williams

Obstinate Orange by Sherwin-Williams

Neighborly Peach by Sherwin-Williams

Marmalade by Benjamin Moore

Carrot Stick by Benjamin Moore

Melon Popsicle by Benjamin Moore

MY FAVORITE BROWNS

Soho by Ralph Lauren

Chocolate Souffle by Ralph Lauren

Traditional by Ralph Lauren

Java by Benjamin Moore

Firewood by Benjamin Moore

Chocolate Mousse by Benjamin Moore

Chocolate Sundae by Benjamin Moore

Turkish Coffee by Sherwin-Williams

MY FAVORITE YELLOWS

Trinket by Sherwin-Williams

American Cheese by Benjamin Moore

Lemon Meringue by Benjamin Moore

Lemon Drops by Benjamin Moore

Lemon Soufflé by Benjamin Moore

Crème Fraiche by Benjamin Moore

Sunburst by Benjamin Moore

Yellow by Benjamin Moore

RED Red is not a color for the faint of heart but rather for those with plenty of heart. The use of red is a strong choice that exudes confidence, and that confidence transcends all cultures. It is not by coincidence that nearly every country's flag contains some red; it's a color that announces itself and makes its presence known. But there is no fence-sitting with red; either you do it or you don't.

ORANGE Whether it's the vibrancy of a tangerine, the lusciousness of an inviting peach, or the homespun warmth of a pumpkin, orange can be very anchoring when found in rugs, tapestries, vessels, paintings— and especially flowers.

BROWN Brown is sexy simply because it is earthy; it's from whence we came and where we'll return. I have always found it to be one of the most useful colors, as it can be interpreted as high glamour or traditional simplicity depending on what you pair it with: think chocolate with periwinkle, or chartreuse for more whimsical styles, or mahogany with emerald, or ruby for formal settings.

YELLOW With yellow, always stay close to colors found in nature and avoid those used to signal CAUTION or YIELD or NO PARKING HERE. Yellows are magical in rooms where we gather, because they lend themselves to light, life, and family.

MY FAVORITE GRAYS

Bunny Gray by Benjamin Moore

Thundercloud Gray by Benjamin Moore

Gray Timber Wolf by Benjamin Moore

Smoke Embers by Benjamin Moore

Lily White by Benjamin Moore

Charcoal Slate by Benjamin Moore

Sea Life by Benjamin Moore

Gravel Gray by Benjamin Moore

MY FAVORITE GREENS

Dark Celery by Benjamin Moore

Limeade Green by Ralph Lauren

Pear Green by Benjamin Moore

Wales by Benjamin Moore

Celadon Green by Benjamin Moore

Sassy Green by Sherwin-Williams

Hearts of Palm by Sherwin-Williams

Saguaro by Sherwin-Williams

MY FAVORITE BLUES

Blue Nova by Benjamin Moore

Prussian Blue by Ralph Lauren

Starry Night Blue by Benjamin Moore

Windmill Wings by Benjamin Moore

Blue Hydrangea by Benjamin Moore

Blue Daisy by Benjamin Moore

Blue Lapis by Benjamin Moore

Turquoise Powder by Benjamin Moore

MY FAVORITE PURPLES

Peace and Happiness by Benjamin Moore

Dewberry by Sherwin-Williams

Academy Purple by Ralph Lauren

Amethyst Stone by Ralph Lauren

Wishing Well by Benjamin Moore

Spring Purple by Benjamin Moore

Ash Violet by Sherwin-Williams

Lavender Mist by Benjamin Moore

GRAY Gray is brown's misunderstood little sister. She is moody, not gloomy, and in the home looks instantly important, creating a sense of timelessness. Achieve a more masculine look with menswear gray flannel—or go more feminine with silk in a shade of black South Sea pearl. Don't choose gray to be safe; choose it to be distinctive.

GREEN The abundance of green outdoors makes it one of the most neutral colors, so if you are looking for a sure thing, green is the way to go. From the palest tone of a lettuce heart to the muddy hue of a magnolia leaf, green is a life color, and will always feed the soul.

BLUE I am always drawn to blue's expansive allure. My two most memorable bedrooms were both blue: one was a heavenly shade of sky with a hint of pale teal; the other a moody Wedgwood. I rarely had a sleepless night in either (unless by choice).

PURPLE The color purple originally signified royalty, and that may be true, but purple in its vast range of shades is a color that is emotional and entrancing. Saturated purples look undeniably regal in formal spaces. Used in a bedroom, lavender can be contemplative and soothing. Choose lacquered aubergine for a candlelit dining room and you are talking high drama. How can you not adore a color that's found in violet skies and Elizabeth Taylor's eyes.

GREEN GROWS MY CARRIAGE HOUSE

When Tom and I moved to New Orleans several years ago, we needed to find a place to live while we went back and forth from our apartment in New York City. We had the good fortune of crossing paths with friends of friends who had a wonderful nineteenth-century carriage house available. It took just one look at the place for us to fall in love with the simple rustic structure that gave us more space than we were used to in my prewar building on the Upper East Side. But what was most enchanting and what sealed the clearly meant-to-be deal was the original brick floor. Some of the bricks still bore the stamp of the owner's initials from the plantation where the bricks were made. Although I don't know of any plantation in my family's history, the initials were that of my late father's. Fate had stepped in.

As we began to make the space our home, we knew we wanted to bring indoors the lushness of the semitropical foliage surrounding the house outside. We painted the focal wall of the oversized living area a great shade of Benjamin Moore Dark Celery to create immediate warmth and intimacy. To some, green may seem like a bold color statement, but I saw it as a strong neutral because it's so natural. I especially loved it with the earthy browns found in our wood furniture, distressed leather, and natural hides we used throughout the room. We painted the rest of the space a soft café au lait and the adjacent dining room a fabulous, high-gloss chocolate brown. I wanted the long, narrow dining room to feel dramatic under candlelight, and the chocolate icing color played beautifully off of the crisp leaf green wall.

As an accent, we once again looked to the aged brick floors for inspiration. Wonderful warm tones of orange and peach in them led us to choose just the right orange chinoiserie chandelier for a reading nook and vibrant tomato red contemporary paintings by our friend Bryan Burkey created visual balance on the opposite wall. Once we established a basic color scheme for our home, our jobs as decorators only became easier: rooms started to take on a life of their own, and decisions about the color palette seemed to make themselves. A small, delightful Rosenthal ceramic wall hanging, purchased by my parents in Europe in the

OPPOSITE *A vintage armchair from Jon Vaccari Design and a groovy glass-topped coffee table from Hazelnut add a mid-century vibe to my traditional space.*

sixties, was the obvious piece of art to hang on our new green wall, as it possessed all the colors that were coming together in the room. We naturally gravitated to an easy-to-maintain and affordable chocolate ultra-suede to reupholster a mid-century modern "Dick Van Dyke" sofa I found at Salvation Army. We chose the perfect rugs made of patched cowhide skins and ethnic wools. Adding hints of gold in tables and lamps from Hazelnut gave that ever-needed gleam of metallic. There may seem to be a whole lot of color going on—and indeed there is—but the heavy dose of neutrals through-out both rooms kept everything grounded and inviting. And not to fear, if that celery green had not worked, we would have just changed it . . . it's only paint.

ABOVE *A recently unearthed Rosenthal is an attic acquisition.*

OPPOSITE *Tom's hand-blown glass bowl by Siemon Caleb sits well with some of our favorite travel treasures that we brought back from our vacation to Thailand: antique carved puppet heads and a persimmon Jim Thompson silk pillow.*

Sally and Richard Edrington's Cottage
COLOR OUTSIDE THE LINES

One of the most successful uses of color that I have ever seen is designer Melissa Rufty's work in Sally and Richard Edrington's vibrant and lively Garden District cottage in New Orleans. Sally is one of the most effervescent, big-hearted personalities I know. Her energy and spirit are contagious—there is nothing beige or monotone about her. She revels in color, and using it in every nook and cranny of her home works for her, because it mirrors her life. Melissa successfully captured Sally's distinctive personality in every room in a project that was a perfect marriage between a client with a true passion for color and a designer with the skill and talent to pull it all off. A home should honestly reflect the style and desires of the owner, and this wonderful house is all Sally, although she will argue right back that it is all Melissa. It is a great testament to a perfect pairing.

That color plays together in a magical way is clearly evident when you enter the front parlor. The backdrop of the living room and dining room is Benjamin Moore's

Linen White against which a clever interplay of the primary colors yellow, blue, and red reigns supreme. The canary yellow ball-gown silk drapes in luscious Pierre Frey satin amplify the sunny disposition of the home owner. Light and happiness stream in from these dazzling windows. The French blue in the living room rug anchors the room, as do the sensuous azure silk velvet sofa and the cowhide antique side chairs, while the confident use of red for art and accessories gives the entire room a "wow" factor. Let's face it, this room started off white, but it would never be described as such.

The design story here is one of joy and personality, balance and harmony, achieved through masterful layering and repetition of the three primary colors. A less artful designer may have used color without restraint, but Melissa carefully chose a mix of vibrant colors that would live together in a dynamic way. As fabulous as they are, the yellow window treatments would easily have dominated the room if the designer had retreated from color rather than balanced it with a deliberate use of bold hues. In the dining room, a large, contemporary crimson painting and a lacquered red Asian buffet are the perfect dance partners for those ballroom drapes. Yellow, so prominent at the windows both in color

OPPOSITE *Andrew Bucci watercolors, pillows made from Dragon Empress fabric from Clarence House, and the bold glass bowl by famed artist Borek Sitek (that Sally found in Prague) celebrate primary colors with a sophisticated twist.*

and design (I adore the Asian reference in the quilted pagoda tipped cornices), shows up again only in subtle ways: a more acidy hue appears in the living room in the striking print on one antique chair and a tiny leather taboret, and vases in the dining room. Red, the costar color, pops up again in the painting in the dining room, as well as in the rug and accent pillows and the whimsical glass bowl on the coffee table. Various shades of blue actually complete the dance card and make the room feel unified and relaxing. The blue found in the

sumptuous velvet sofa also graces pillows, the Oriental rug, and a hide-covered accent chair. And I love the way blue flows right into the dining room on the back of each chair in that wonderful distressed leather. One of my favorite touches is the subtle use of deep blue paint lightly outlining the citron-hued chair—like a worn patina. I think the color story in this room is perfect. The bounty of color comes together masterfully and draws you in, while the complex mix begs you to stay and play all day.

2

SAVE SOME FUN FOR LATER

What I love about decorating is not just enjoying the finished product but also immersing myself in the creative process. I never want my rooms to feel finished; decorating should be continuous. If you do everything at once, you will just end up with a staged set (and I love sets, but I don't want to live in one!), not a home that reflects you. When we are living our lives right, we are growing every day. The same applies to your décor.

HOME WASN'T BUILT IN A DAY

TIP Enlisting the help of a designer, of course, is a wise way to jump-start the decorating process and to accomplish a great deal in a timely manner. It is also smart to utilize expertise that you may not possess—let's face it, not everyone has the time to create a perfect floor plan or a super-chic color palette. A good designer should love the process and be passionate about guiding you to develop your own style. Be wary of anyone who insists that you do everything in a formulaic way.

OVERLEAF *A butterfly-themed collection is fresh and cool in this indigo and silver vignette.*

ABOVE *The shell and china collections couldn't be more different in theme, but when artfully displayed together, their unifying thread of tangerine and white makes a strong decorative statement.*

OPPOSITE *I am mesmerized by the stellar collection of Chihuly glass, especially the fluidity of the lighted arrangement juxtaposed against the geometric chest.*

As we grow and mature, so do our likes and dislikes. I take great pleasure in adding things to my décor over time—tweaking what works, spicing things up with fabrics or accessories, and creating my own personal history. I am always looking for new ways to have fun with decoration, and to keep the party going. My favorite way, one that I began cultivating as a young child, comes in the form of passionate collecting.

Collecting allows your love of design to grow over decades. By its very nature it can become a constant in your life while you develop your sense of style. Collections—whether books, art, seashells, or ceramics—help to define the personality of the room and tell the story of who you are, where you have been, and what tickles your fancy. And these cherished items will move effortlessly with you from home to home, like a loyal best friend.

Of course, collections have to be edited and styled—I am not talking about piles of clutter or layers of knickknacks that take up every square inch of space, leaving no place for your eyes to rest. I am talking about your own sentimental attachment to certain objects, the ones hand-carried home from traveling abroad, inherited from a beloved family member, or plucked with your discerning eye for their hidden potential from a favorite consignment shop. Your

motivation for each acquisition should simply be how the object speaks to you on an emotional level, not how much it is worth. The value in the sentiment behind what only you can gather for display far exceeds the value of the lot.

I'm always amazed at what people are drawn to and what they collect. Some people collect boxes, some collect figurines. Some are concerned about building an important collection of antique furniture or acquiring significant art, and some keep it simple with whimsical pottery or a special porcelain pattern. Other collections are quirky and highly imaginative and kitschy. The possibilities are as endless. Collecting not only nourishes your soul, but also gives others a clear picture of what your interests are, what kind of sense of humor you possess, and what is unique about your personality. Whatever and however you collect, follow your heart.

KEEP IT NEAT For years, I have actively haunted junk shops, vintage stores, and flea markets searching for stylish 1960s barware, shakers, and unusually colored glasses. As each martini glass or goblet joins my troupe, new memories unfold. And, if nothing else, drinks certainly taste better when stylishly served!

OPENING NIGHT

On my first birthday, my grandmother gave me a sterling silver wine goblet, and thereafter, she gave me one every year until I had a complete dozen. As a toddler, I found the shiny vessels so bright and inviting, and although by the age of five I secretly wanted Hot Wheels, I was very charmed by my grandmother's lovely tradition—and thus, my collector mentality was born.

When I moved to New York after college, this tradition carried on with every engraved silver mint julep cup my mother and family friends gave me to celebrate my Broadway show openings. I now have quite a beautiful collection of silver julep cups and goblets. I adore each of them and, although they have seen their share of adult refreshments, I also use them in a multitude of capacities: as toothbrush holders, desk accessories, and bud vases that hold tiny floral arrangements lined up and down the center of my dining room table. These beautiful little vessels have proudly joined every apartment and home I have inhabited, fondly reminding me of my grandmother, mother, and friends, as well as every joyous opening night (even if the show flopped, I still ended up with an award!).

OPPOSITE *Just like at a great family reunion, my grandfather's 1930s sterling martini shaker plays nicely with my grandmother's silver goblets and mint julep cups. The invited guests, my 1960s vintage barware, serve as buffers, should there be any dispute.*

LOVE THAT BOOTY

Long ago, while I was on the road with *Cats,* whenever time allowed I'd hit every antiques auction and junk shop possible in every city, town, and tiny burg where we performed, gathering treasures that to this day are still a part of my home. Things would catch my eye that reminded me of home or of the home I would one day have. Whimsical, humorous collectibles captured my imagination, and art was always something I simply had to have. My most prized collection is the art I have accumulated since my first purchase at age twelve. By no means is it worth a vast fortune, nor will it overly impress, but I love my collection and do not regret one purchase to this date. As I look back, my only regrets are the pieces that for some reason got away.

As far back as my awkward early teen-age years, I started feeding my passion for hunting and gathering "cool stuff" to create my own special look within my parents' home. Armed with the Sunday newspaper, I'd circle antique auctions, estate sales, and yard sales, and use manual labor as a bargaining tool so that my mom or dad would play chauffer. While this interest was blossoming, my parents were building their dream house, and I reveled in their planning, eagerly participating in conversa-

tions and field trips to source the custom millwork, handcrafted hardware, fixtures, and paint colors, all of which trained my eye to seek out good design. From that point on I was hooked, and hunting for special treasures became as natural as breathing. I left no stone unturned, checking out every possible avenue, both the high and the low end. Countless hours were spent in the finest antiques stores, art galleries, and museums just learning all I could about the decorative arts and cultivating my own sense of style. And over the years, I have found many sources for affordable collecting that have kept me returning for successful hunts.

MY GREATEST HITS

There are meccas of thrift and consignment stores, auction houses, art galleries, and antiques and retail shops in the three cities where I now live—New York, Los Angeles, and New Orleans. Allow me to share my favorite haunts.

OPPOSITE *When I cast the characters for my bedroom wall, works had to be black, white, gray, or gold to make the cut. It is truly a mixed-media wall, in both subject matter and form. Among my favorites are Skylar Fein's "Batman on Poppers" and a photograph of me by Timothy White from a* Playboy *magazine fashion shoot.*

NEW YORK CITY: A HELL OF A TOWN

At every turn, this city is truly a feast for the eyes. Every neighborhood has its own design point of view, imaginative retailers, and great art at every price point.

- **Housing Works** thrift store cannot be beat for a plethora of fantastic treasures. Whenever I change direction in décor, I donate to this organization, which helps people with HIV and AIDS.
- Visiting the **26th Street Flea Market** is a standing tradition whenever I'm in town. I scour this market for chic retro barware.
- **Doyle New York**, an auction house on East Eighty-seventh Street, is always my pick when I'm looking to expand my art collection.
- **Art Student Showcase**, in SoHo, features the works of up-and-coming artists. Its proprietor, Paul Toler, is extremely personable and has a wealth of knowledge—there's no snobby art vibe here.
- I go to East Sixtieth Street for exquisite uptown antiques, and then beeline to Elizabeth Street in Nolita for divine downtown design.
- **Bergdorf Goodman** offers cutting-edge, high-glam home furnishings mixed with classic, luxurious collections. Just walking through the halls and rooms is a great way to get inspired by the talents of this venerable retailer.

LOS ANGELES: TALES OF TINSELTOWN

I love the West Coast vibe, an exhilarating fusion of Hollywood glamour meets elegant, laid-back living.

- The **Rose Bowl Flea Market** is the grand dame of outdoor flea markets and is the only way to spend the second Sunday of the month.
- The **Melrose Trading Post**, a flea market held on Sundays in the parking lot of Fairfax High School at the corner of Melrose and Fairfax, charges only two dollars for admission, a small price to pay for so many finds.
- **Blackman Cruz, Eccola,** and **Bourgeois Bohème** are temples of design with a mind-boggling mix of antique, vintage, and mid-century modern furnishings—browsing these stores is just short of a carnal experience (upon exiting I often feel like having a cigarette).
- **Hollyhock** and **Leif** are two superb shops in the West Hollywood area. Upon entering, I am immediately lulled into their exquisite world of chic and always find some of the most impressive displays of furniture, lighting, and accessories I've ever seen.
- **Bonhams & Butterfields** on Sunset Boulevard is a wonderful auction house with a worldwide reputation.

There is nothing quite like the inherent jazz and pizzazz that is New Orleans.

- **The French Quarter** is home to spectacular antiques shops. And just strolling though the ancient narrow streets is a visually moving experience. Beneath the wrought-iron balconies and among the decaying patina of the colorful walls, one instantly feels as if they have entered another world.

- **M. S. Rau Antiques, Moss Antiques, Royal Antiques,** and **Keil's Antiques** feature one-of-a-kind pieces worthy of museums. The proprietors have been in the business for generations and are always on hand to impart their expertise.

- **Wirthmore Antiques, Karla Katz and Co., Balzac Antiques,** and **Uptowner Antiques** have been my faves for years. Designers flock to these Magazine Street beacons in droves.

- **Perch, Shadyside Pottery, Lūm Vintage Lighting,** and **Jon Vaccari Design** feature, respectively, the best in furnishings and fabric, handmade raku and stoneware vessels, unique lighting and drop-dead gorgeous furniture.

- **Cole Pratt Gallery, Kevin Gillentine Gallery, Jonathan Ferrara Gallery,** and **Arthur Roger Gallery** showcase the finest art in town. I love "sipping and seeing" at the new exhibit openings, which take place on the first Saturday of every month.

- **Retroactive** and **Neophobia** satisfy my desire for anything retro. Retroactive has one of the most extensive stashes of sixties barware and objets d'art, not to mention vintage clothing, cuff links, and jewelry worthy of visits from the *Mad Men* costume designers.

- **Renaissance Interiors** in the nearby suburb of Metairie is far and away my favorite consignment shop. I can kill two birds with one stone here, dropping off my own edited wares, while scoring some new treasures.

- The **New Orleans Academy of Fine Arts** has several student art shows a year, and I have shopped here consistently in support of emerging talent.

- **New Orleans Auction** and **Neal Auction Company** have been my stomping grounds since college.

TIP I particularly love to support local artists. It reinforces and nurtures a sense of home, and it is a great way to celebrate your own town through your décor. One of my favorite pieces was given to me by my sweet mother as a Christmas gift: a mid-century painting (circa 1966) by New Orleans artist Dell Weller. The oil on Masonite perfectly depicts a moody, blue-hued French Quarter and Le Petit Théâtre, the jewel box of a theater where I got my start and, like my mother did, I now serve on the board of directors. It's a sentimental journey every time I glance at it.

GIFTS THAT
KEEP ON GIVING

One of the best ways to add to your collection and at the same time generously support a favorite charitable organization is to frequent benefit auctions. Every city and many small towns have them. Whether silent bidding, paddle raising, or white-glove waving, you can help raise money for worthy causes at a multitude of different charitable events while also feathering your nest.

For years I have hosted benefit auctions and chaired galas in New York, New Orleans, and L.A., where art and collectibles are the featured attraction. The year after Hurricane Katrina, my wonderful friend Ti Martin and I were the chairs for Art Against AIDS in New Orleans. It was the first gala in the newly renovated and reopened Ritz Carlton, and with the help of everyone at the NO/AIDS Task Force, we did everything possible to make this commemorative event stellar. Ti, being a member of the famed Brennan restaurant dynasty and co-owner of Commander's Palace, made calls to all her chef friends across the country and was able to procure dozens of first-edition and autographed

A TIP ABOUT AUCTIONS I enjoy the thrill of a live auction, but I prefer leaving a silent bid, which works well since I travel so much and often cannot attend on the auction date. Anyone can request a catalogue from an auction house, which serves to bring big city art to any small town. Although I'm not a gambler per se, leaving or sending in my bid provides a similar thrill, and when I get lucky, I'm able to add a wonderful work of art or piece of great furniture to my collection.

cookbooks for a live auction lot. Meanwhile, I contacted and e-mailed everyone I knew in show business. Tickets to Broadway shows and live television tapings came pouring in. My friend and multi–Tony Award winner Tommy Tune generously donated one of his own original works of art. As I emceed the live auction, working furiously to get the bids higher and higher, I was too focused to see who was landing the best of the lot, but at the end of a fabulous and emotional evening, it warmed my heart to learn that my brother, Jay, bought Tommy Tune's butterfly piece for my nieces, Bailey and Kelly, and that my partner, Tom, was going home with those cookbooks!

CLOCKWISE FROM TOP LEFT: *These are a few of my favorite finds: an artist's proof by famed illustrator Alexander Sharpe Ross from Doyle New York, faceted crystal ball drawer pulls from Melrose Trading Post, Del Weller's Vieux Carre painting from New Orleans Auction, and a handmade whimsical bird sculpture from Hazelnut atop signed cookbooks.*

WALL OF SHAME

In my family home, on the walls of a very long hallway, my mother decided to hang a multitude of photographs. Searching through boxes where she kept old and some newer pictures of family and friends, she found the good, the bad, and the ugly—and by that I mean the fun nudies of babies on bearskin rugs, my grandmothers' wedding portraits from the Roaring Twenties, dance recital pictures, Little League team shots, formal studio photographs of family members, some of my parents at dinner dances during their courting days, and everything in between. It clearly told the story of our past and present. My mother had each photograph custom framed, and the "Wall of Shame," as she jokingly called it, was born. The wall turned out to be an ongoing and growing project, and she cleverly and intentionally left space for future additions, for the new family members and friends as they were welcomed into our lives . . . saving some fun for later. As much as my family loved this corridor, it also turned out to be the place in her home where guests congregated for a look and conversation.

As I ventured out into the world on my own, I instinctively re-created a version of the Wall of Shame in every residence thereafter. I found that the effect can still be achieved at a moderate cost by using premade frames in the same color or style; I always choose one uniform color, such as classic black lacquer or, my favorite, gold leaf. I've collected so many gold leaf frames over the years—probably more than is necessary—but when the right photo is married to the perfect gold frame and hung on my wall, it's really a match made in heaven.

You Oughta Be in Pictures The concept of displayed portrait ancestry is rooted in the grand châteaus of France, the royal villas of Italy, and the great manors of England. It was common among the aristocracy, but you don't need to be a duke or duchess to have a real painted portrait. Photography is fantastic for capturing an exact moment in time, and although it is a respected art form, your Olan Mills high school portrait can't compare to what an artist's hand can create. When I was a child, my mother would often take me to Jackson Square (a hub for artists—almost every community has one) to look at the local artists' portraiture. I still have the fun silhouettes, colorful pastels, charcoals, pencil drawings, serious oils, and even caricatures of yours truly. Maybe one day, if it doesn't appear too egomaniacal, I'll display the collection, perhaps in a powder room or, more appropriately, in the basement or the lowly mudroom.

I adore our family collection of portraits, from the formal oils to crayon spoofs. The exquisite pencil drawing of my nieces by gifted New Orleans artist Nancy Dawes (center), my Sardi's charicature (far left), and the images of my mother and brother (far right) that I colored and painted myself just make me happy.

LET IT ALL HANG OUT

Not all collections have to be displayed on your walls—or even at all. They can be private, but I believe that what you choose to collect and display says something about you. What makes one person's treasures more interesting and alluring than another's really boils down to how the collection is presented, which will most reflect your personal style. How you decide to group your favorite things together should relate to the rest of your decorative scheme. Rather than some careless, random scattering, strive for an artful arrangement that enhances the overall impact of each piece and has a well-focused point of view.

Once you get your collection going (and you don't have to wait for it to be complete, as there is no such thing), you can begin to stack and group your finds in clever ways that empower each item with even greater decorative value than it might otherwise have on its own. Think carefully about how to group objects together for the greatest visual impact or hang art in a way to draw interest to the pieces in an unexpected manner.

Collections that are grouped by color can work wonderfully for items that run the price-range gamut. A vast collection of creamware pottery when bunched together, for example, will pack a far greater punch than displaying a single plate or two

ABOVE *Paintings and a winged wall sculpture hang in a relaxed organic style that exudes spirit and charm in this artist's cottage.*

OPPOSITE *A vast collection of white pottery and ceramic creamware is tightly grouped for maximum monochromatic decorative effect.*

willy-nilly around the room. I have a friend who for years has collected art glass in every funky shade of green imaginable. Displayed together, the pieces resonate with saturated hues of emerald as light catches all the various shapes and sizes.

There is no hard and fast rule for how to group art. Find a formation you like, or one that will support your collection. Try a regimented grid, a symmetrical arrangement, a style that follows the lines of an archway or door, or even a free-form installation. Remember, it has to look pleasing to your eye, and keep in mind that walls are strong: they can hold more than one painting. Just don't overdo it and lose track of the wall's overall focus. We all need to locate and become good friends with our inner edit button, making sure it is on and working at all times. But I cannot stress enough to trust your instinct: *if it looks right, it is right.*

I love stacking my art and mixing up the types of art mediums in the display for texture. The display is linear and ordered, and, most importantly, it can tell a story. A sunburst mirror above or even below a couple of paintings always works to my eye and is the perfect exclamation point.

Small pieces can appear more important and grander in a big frame or oversized matte; have fun playing with the proportions. The same goes for mixing and matching modern works with antique ornate frames. Keep an open mind, and try taking

a less-traveled road—you may discover something new and wonderful in something you already have.

MY SIGNATURE COLLECTION

I have been a fan of Laurel Wilder's art glass plates for years. In fact, when Tom and I opened Hazelnut, works by her and her lovely sister Shelley were the first we wanted to feature. Using a reverse decoupage technique—hand stamped with gold leaf, then sealed, signed, and numbered—each work is unique and food safe, so they are not only gorgeous but also functional. I knew that custom plates celebrating the beauty and history of New Orleans would be a sensation, so a friend photographed the iconic fountain in Audubon Park and I sifted through my collection of antique maps, copies of *Harper's Weekly* depicting historic scenes of Mardi Gras, and Audubon prints of Gulf Coast birds. I then called Shelley, and together we designed a collection of plates that are elegant and dazzling when displayed.

I love the graceful allure of the Audubon Muse plate just as much as I cherish our plate that celebrates the Flambeaux carriers with their fiery torches lighting up the night sky. More recently, we've created plates inspired by the majestic pelicans, egrets, and herons that have survived the 2010 oil spill in the Gulf. They remind me of great beauty and strength.

OPPOSITE *Katy's collection of Laurel Wilder platters displayed on the wall is a perfect complement to her living room's strict gold and green palette. Sentimental favorites are the trays inspired by antique maps of Vieux Carré, flambeau carriers, and* Harper's Weekly *images of the first Mardi Gras tableau.*

ABOVE *The Audubon Muse plate.*

My Batt Cave
BEDROOM EYES

I was flattered to be asked by *House Beautiful* to participate in its "Why I Love My Bed" feature. Although by then our carriage house had been photographed for the *New York Times* and *Southern Accents,* my bedroom had never been photographed, mainly because it was still a "work in progress." This was the perfect opportunity to refine the space, and we had just one month before the shoot. The paint color was Benjamin Moore's Smoke Embers—a sophisticated shade of gray—and is serene, masculine, and calming. The accents were antique gold; natural wood; and black, but the walls were pretty bare. They stood at attention waiting for adornment.

I quickly called my dear friend Suzie Allain, a noted artist and designer, to commission a work that would hang over our bed. I had come to adore her emotional oils of scenes depicting drying bamboo on moody, gray grounds. And then, like a whirling dervish, I began to unearth my paintings, prints, drawings, and sketches that I had collected over the years just waiting for their star turn. Many were already framed in pretty vintage gold frames or simple black ones (a decision I made along the way so they would be unified in any installation).

My collection is extremely eclectic, accumulated over three decades. As I perused the works, I was flooded with

many happy memories of how each piece had been acquired. It was like running into long-lost friends and reminiscing. I realized that almost my entire hidden collection could completely adorn one wall, making an enormous visual and emotional impact.

My eyes were drawn to one little print I had purchased while in the seventh grade on Royal Street. It is a Charles Bragg rendering of a bat, or "flying mouse," titled "Die Fledermaus" (being that my surname is Batt, I had to have it!). I had held on to that cute little rat for more than thirty

years, and now he would graduate with honors to our bedroom wall. And over the course of the next couple of weeks, the room came together beautifully, as each cherished piece found its place of honor. I literally wallpapered the entire wall with our personal history.

The photo shoot was a success, and when we bought a new home, one decision was definite: our room would be re-created and morphed to fit the space. This time, there was no need to start over. When something works, let it be!

3

THE MIX: SHAKEN AND STIRRED

Just like the perfect dinner party, the success of a room depends upon the mix. The best way to ensure sparkling conversation and witty repartee is to always include a sprinkling of personalities with varied backgrounds. Introducing new people to your group will bring fresh views and ideas and will inspire personal growth. Think of your décor in the same way: a great mix of styles that is flexible and continuously evolving. This philosophy will keep your interiors alive.

DO THE TWIST

Shaken or stirred, it's the art of blending that is imperative in creating distinctive and dynamic spaces. The ability to look at many different styles, materials, and periods with an open mind and to uniquely meld them together gives vibrancy and energy to interior design. Strictly adhering to a formula or one period is not only confining, but it is also one note that doesn't really sing. You may enjoy monastery sculpture, but let's face it, you don't really want to live in a monastery. Same goes for completely period rooms: although I adore visiting the decorative arts exhibits at the Metropolitan Museum of Art, I don't want to live there. We can gracefully nod to the past while living completely in the here and now.

I think "the mix" is an inherently American ideology, since we are a nation of so many wonderful cultures. The rich heritage of European, Asian, African, South American, and Middle Eastern styles all come into play with American design. There is great beauty in this diversity. Mixing these sensibilities gives us the opportunity to create an energetic flow in a room, keeping our eyes delightfully moving rather than stopping, settling, and getting bored.

My mother always identified with and adored French antiques, while my father was a complete modernist. My father loved everything to be comfortable and relaxed—the leather sofas in the den were so low and plush that we'd have to send out a rescue line to retrieve sinking visitors. My mother put functionality aside, caring solely for the beauty and artistry of the room (although she did hold fast to her rule that there must always be a chair that a man can sit in without breaking it). Being raised with this dichotomy helped me to appreciate the design elements of both worlds. At an early age, I could identify with the delicate beauty of an exquisitely carved Louis XV chair leg as well as the iconic, streamlined refinement of an Eames chair. However, in my parents' home, the two worlds did not completely mix. Rather, certain rooms were definitely his and others were hers. Expansive, chocolate leather sofas and a massive coffee table inlaid with burled wood and brass were my father's choices for the den. Keeping with the seventies vibe, the walls were covered in cork wallpaper, and the enormous custom rug was camel-hued wool. Against one entire wall

OVERLEAF *An "early attic" Victorian settee earns its stripes sitting beneath a contemporary painting by Amanda Talley against flowering wallpaper by Osborne and Little. Welcome to the mix.*

OPPOSITE *The explosive hues in this Madeline Weinrib fabric, a heartful spin on an ikat, jazzes up a traditional chair.*

was a custom-milled entertainment center where the television ruled the roost. (Thank heaven my mother insisted that doors be attached so it could be hidden at parties.) In the living room, my mother clearly had the upper hand, with pale ivory silk papered walls that lived harmoniously with yards of deep rose–colored velvets and floral silks. Hers was the world of dainty demilune tables, a carved trumeau mirror with cherubs, and ladylike settees paired with ornate cocktail tables. Objets d'art filled the room; think Limoges porcelain, cut crystal Baccarat lamps, and a sterling Buccellati menagerie.

I suppose on some level this arrangement worked for them. But even as a young child, I was dying to run through the rooms and see what might happen if I swapped a silk brocade bergère for a leather wingback recliner, to see how it would look to have a Dresden figurine waltzing atop the green felt of the billiard table. My intense desire to shake things up has remained with me since then.

Trolling for Treasures Thankfully, my lifetime practice of investing in antique and vintage furniture and my appreciation for quirky family hand-me-downs is now all the rage. Scavenging for great finds and imagining ways I can give them a modern twist are my favorite activities. The ultimate eco-friendly way of decorating is to be able to see the potential in existing pieces, visualize their possibilities, refurbish them, and allow them to continue to thrive in your home. New is not necessarily better. In many cases, there is just no way new furnishings can have the character and soul that older items can bring to the mix. Train your eye to see beyond the obvious; a fresh new look is just a costume change away.

ABOVE *A resourceful artist took an antique French plaster remnant, galvanized tin, and pages from old books, and, voilà, a work of art.*

OPPOSITE *Old and new cleverly mix with high and low in an imaginative style. Aged exterior shutters brought inside serve as a backdrop for a classic camelback sofa, modern Saarinen coffee table, and antique mercury glass pharmacy bottles. Argentine pelts and chartreuse silk pillows add texture and pop.*

EVERYTHING OLD IS NEW AGAIN

There is something so refreshing about combining old things with new; I suppose it's because each helps to define what is beautiful about the other and enhances one another's charm. One tried-and-true combination that always delivers is hanging very progressive and vibrant contemporary art near classic antiques. You can also try this mix of old-with-new eras using fabrics, rugs, and accessories. An iconic modernist Barcelona chair looks even sexier when sitting on a threadbare antique Oushak rug, and an ornately carved antique chair looks fantastic reupholstered in a modern geometric print. Opposites do attract, and when the combination is right, it's eye catching.

One of my favorite pastimes is to scour junk shops and flea markets for architectural fragments, such as bits from old columns or pieces from old pediments, and then refabricate them for a new purpose. I love the way the patina shows through the many layers of paint and gilt that only time can bring. These richly designed and beautifully carved works can be easily turned into great sconces or lamps (a talented craftsperson can help you with this), or sometimes I simply hang them as art. It is so much fun to imagine them in their original incarnations and to see them rewired or outfitted for a present-day use.

BOY MEETS GIRL

In my book, adhering to gender roles in decorating is quite narrow and passé. I love to see uber-masculine Napoleonic Empire furniture with ormolu, which looks like medals on an admiral's chest, coupled with the palest of lavender silk drapes or softly painted walls. A delicate, curlicue-carved French chair looks so sexy and young upholstered in black leather or a manly velvet animal print. And imagine how fantastic a balletic chandelier dripping with glistening crystals would look dancing above a weighty and massive limestone slab of a dining table. Just like in college, let's have a mixer; you never know who you'll meet.

EAST MEETS WEST

I adored my grandparents, both sets, though they were vastly different. While one pair's aesthetic was a few cross-stitches away from a "Home Sweet Home" sampler and a portrait of Thomas Jefferson, the other was happy with a Buddha and Balinese lamps. My mother's parents, PaPa and Moozie, loved New Orleans, their home, and every aspect of home life. They adored antiques and mixed Federal with Victorian with Colonial, a clearly western viewpoint and a

OPPOSITE *The yang of the masculine oak doors, Flemish painting, and model ship are an elegant marriage to the yin of the feminine nineteenth-century French settee and an ornately carved eighteenth-century Italian console.*

very traditional style. My paternal grand-parents traveled across every ocean to all the corners of the globe, and their taste reflected their vast journeys. Mom-ee and Da-dee appreciated what they saw in the many continents they visited, but they were enraptured with the Orient. Their love for all things Asian was richly apparent in their home décor. This was quite an eyeful growing up, and it fed my fertile imagina-tion. It was never an either/or, but rather an *all,* and I loved it!

HIGH AND LOW

Good design is good design, whether it costs one dollar or ten thousand. A clever combination of both high-end and inexpen-sive pieces brings an energetic and confident look to the room that can only happen when you think beyond price stereotypes. A hefty price tag does not guarantee good taste, and scoring a bargain can often pack a stylish wallop. The value is in the look. There are many pieces of furniture and art that will make you cry when you read your credit card statement, but look at it this way: you will cry only once, and you will have something of great quality that stands the test of time.

It is a good idea to buy the best quality that you can afford so that things last and wear well, but it is also smart to know when you can cut a design corner or two. Everyone deserves a comfortable, appeal-ing place to call home, and creativity and

imagination can often fill in where dollars do not. I felt pretty darn savvy when, instead of purchasing a pair of very pricey mid-century side chairs, I was able to find something quite similar at my favorite consignment shop for one hundred and fifty dollars. I spent a few clams getting them reupholstered in a fun, hip fabric and still had room in the budget to buy the metallic pillows that I had been lusting after. Deco-rating your home need not require a second mortgage. The trick is in squelching your inner snob, and keeping an open mind.

More than ever before, good design is readily available to everyone. Many talented designers have done great work for large store chains and catalogues without sacrific-ing design integrity, helping to make a heightened sense of style accessible to all.

SEE ME, FEEL ME, TOUCH ME

One of the most sophisticated ways to create a subtle mix in your décor is to layer textures, prints, and finishes throughout, which adds to the overall richness and depth of the look. Whether you use the same color or a rainbow of hues in a room, it is critical that the surfaces have contrast, so that the texture of each is visually stimulating. Nothing looks better than high-gloss moldings and trim against

OPPOSITE *With reflective mirror, glass, Lucite, and metallics, this living room remains open and bright.*

eggshell or matte walls; the contrasting finishes give the detail of the wood prominence and focus. High-gloss lacquer is another way to go for a dramatic wall finish. Light reflects in the layers of pigment, creating a great treatment that takes the room up a notch. I love to merge rugged textures with more refined ones, a contrast that helps to amp up the visual content of both and creates a relaxed but chic vibe. I am also crazy for the sheen of rich, silky-satin drapes paired with the nubby, earthy texture of a sea-grass or sisal rug, or yards of beefy Belgian linen hanging against lacquered walls as shiny as a mirror. I can't get enough textural play. I just love it, love it, love it.

BLINDED BY THE LIGHT

Every stylish room must make use of my favorite backup singers: sheen, shimmer, and shine. Mirrors, glass, and metals are indispensable mixers for adding sparkle, glamour, and life to any décor. They reflect light so well and make our living spaces dance. I am not suggesting you hang groupings of disco balls, but I do believe that every room benefits from the endless gift of mirrors. Besides reflecting our image and light, they capture the colors and textures of the room from different vantage points. I love mirrors because they create illusions and are mysterious and magical. What really rocks my world is the moody sparkle and glimmer that can only be found

ABOVE *Blue-and-white patterns at play—no matter how different—always work.*

OPPOSITE *High-gloss walls lacquered in Benjamin Moore's Sepia Tan and a gold-leafed klismos chair shimmer all the more when combined with the rugged texture of a sisal rug and tortoise-shell wall art.*

Heavy on the high with a pinch of low: drapes in Osborne and Little's Showboat fabric, Leontine Linens monogrammed bedding, and charming lime green duvets found on eBay debut in this youthful bedroom.

in antique mirrors. In the aged pixie dust, I see my home and myself differently. These kind surfaces can sometimes soften the ravages of time and will calm your inner Blanche DuBois.

Harness the power of shine though the wonders of transparency with glass, crystal, and Lucite, allowing more light into your life and spaces. These are perfect mediums when used for tables as well as chandeliers and accessories.

Metallics may just be one of my favorite things, and we all could use a good dose of shimmer now and then. They are called precious metals for a good reason. I love the old-world feeling of gold leaf and bronze, as well as the sleek, modern look of layered silver and platinum. Both looks instantly create a sense of opulence and grandeur. From ornate bronze doré to faint touches of antiqued gold or silver painted on the worn patina of an armchair, there is no denying the regal impact metallic can make. Metal is a perfect material for glass-topped cocktail, coffee, and end tables—the combination of the glass and the metal adds light and sheen to the room. Natural steel and brass, dull or polished, are beautiful contrasting metallics. Although some consider silver and gold very different and insist that one should be used without the other, I say mix them: they can both work well in any setting.

ABOVE *The subtle use of gilt in the frame and bookends beneath the glistening amber and crystal chandelier lends a timeless quality to this romantic vignette.*

OPPOSITE *An oversized multipaneled mirror and brass 1940s French chairs upholstered in shiny white patent leather give sophisticated sheen to this old-world bathroom.*

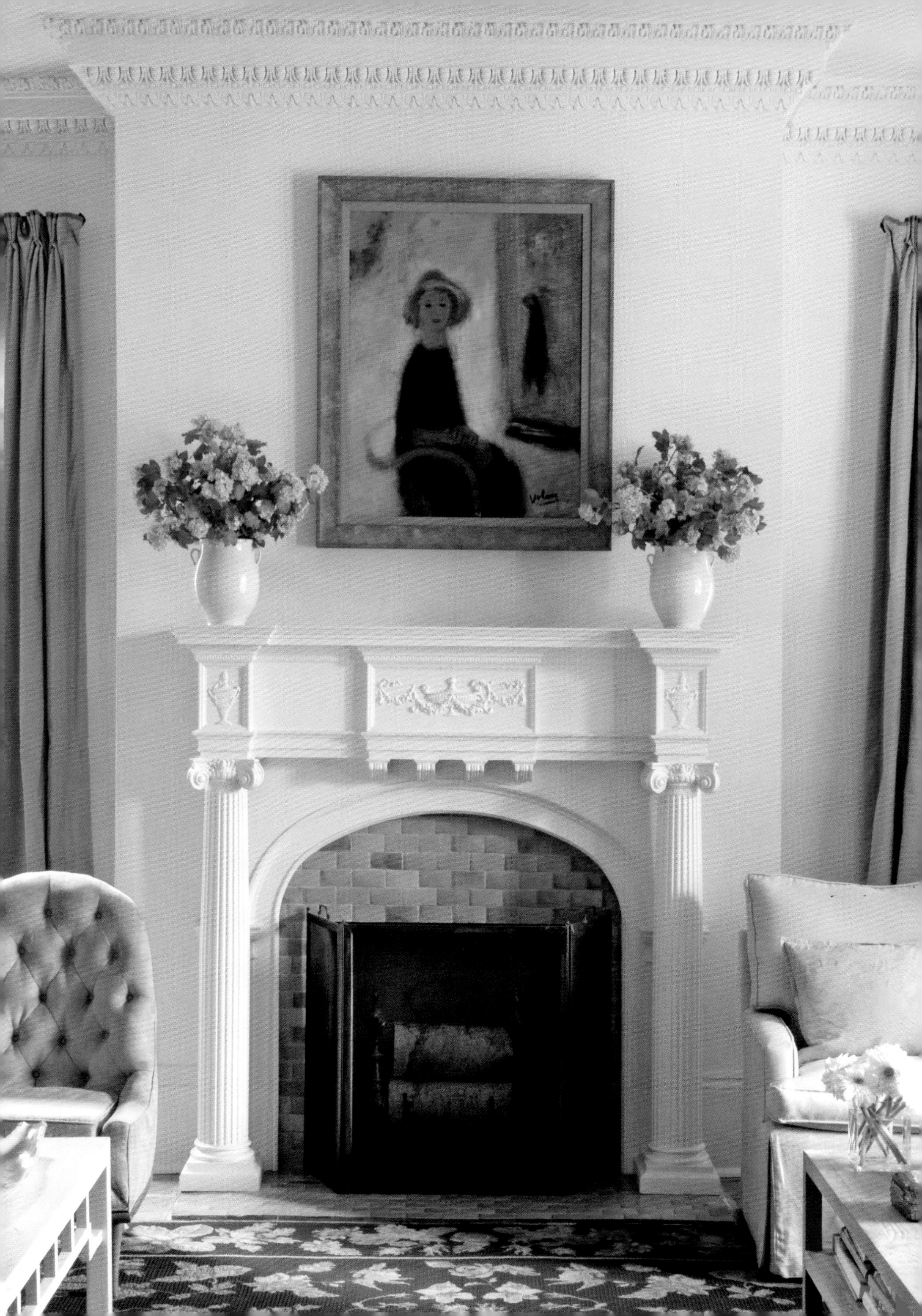

The Friedler Home

MASTERS OF MIXOLOGY

Heidi Friedler, a talented interior designer with an active family, decorated her own home with beautiful furnishings, fabrics, and art all meant to be thoroughly enjoyed. I love that Heidi shuns any rule that declares rooms off-limits or fabrics too precious. She is all about how function can exist without sacrificing the look; all you need is a creative eye. I adore her no-nonsense, no-excuses sense of great style.

The house, with its fabulous architecture and graceful proportions, is the perfect backdrop for Heidi's classic-contemporary American point of view. Under her close and mindful watch, a super-cozy home exists in a lavish setting . . . the epitome of an elegant stylish mix.

Throughout her living room, she has used family heirlooms as a point of departure. The fantastic Portuguese needlepoint rug was her husband Tripp's maternal grandmother's. The 1960s French Vietnamese painting that hangs above the mantel belonged to Tripp's paternal grandmother. The pieces from both sides of the family truly resonate when paired with a fresh approach. Heidi used a green and blue palette, calling out the less obvious tones of green in the rug (rather than the more obvious red) and allowing both grandmothers' pieces to coexist in a charming way.

FAMILY HEIRLOOM TIP For many, decorating a modern space with family heirlooms can prove tricky. When faced with your grandmother's heirlooms, the last thing you want is for your home to look like Maw-Maws "R" Us. I always advise against restaging inherited items as they were in their prime; you'll only be living in the past with a room full of tired old relatives. Bring them into your home with a whole new perspective, and help them take on a new life full of exuberance and emotion. After all, that is what living with sentimental items should really be about . . . living on.

The result is a design that feels current and modern while incorporating and paying homage to the past.

One constant that I adore in the Friedler home is the raw slate floors. The clean gray color of the stone is the perfect unexpected foil to the classic grand moldings and trim. Heidi successfully mixes high and low. Even though she pairs her furniture with such important art in the room, including a contemporary painting, the room never feels too heavy or serious.

Heidi's other smart mixes include:
- A great pair of gold Naugahyde tufted lounge chairs, found on one of her thrift shop hunts, reupholstered in durable taupe suede.
- A colorful vintage ceramic lamp outfitted with a new shade adds a crafty touch.
- Yards and yards of luscious leaf green "silk" drapes that grace the windows, are actually polyester. The sun beating in through these windows would shred silk in minutes, but Heidi, determined not to sacrifice style, created indestructible ball-gown drapes. Now that's ultimate high/low!
- My absolute favorite accent in the room is the pair of antique French Louis XVI chairs, upholstered in sexy blue leather. She inherited those gorgeous chairs just as they are! Besides having great talent, she also has great luck in the hand-me-down department—her grannies really had it going on.

OVERLEAF *Spectacular old-school moldings get a luscious coat of Benjamin Moore's Soft Chamois paint and create a luminous backdrop for a cool blue-green color palette.*

ABOVE AND OPPOSITE *The unexpected combination of accents in this room consists of mixed media works by Allison Stewart, a killer red lamp from Target, and a Robert Gordy portrait hanging next to a Crate and Barrel sofa.*

COLOR AND LIGHT

Suzie Allain and I have been friends since high school. She is an interior designer and a mother of two fabulous teenagers. Her home is decorated in her signature relaxed but sophisticated style that richly demonstrates her vibrant creative talent as well as her confidence in creating an easy yet sophisticated mix. She is my design touchstone.

Suzie painted her living room—walls and all the moldings and trim—in Benjamin Moore Patriotic White. She chose a pearl finish to allow plenty of light to reflect in the rooms, defining a clean and modern palette. The contemporary approach of leaving the windows uncluttered and undressed allows the beautifully aged shutters, with a wonderful blue patina, to take center stage. The living room receives gorgeous northern light, so why cover them up? Let the sunshine in! Suzie then collected an unexpected eclectic mix of high and low furnishings and accessories, both in price and look, to encourage a natural vibe throughout the living room. An angular sofa from Jonathan Adler, upholstered in a slubby ivory tweed, contrasts nicely with the glamorous Oly mirrored round gold-metallic end tables.

The wing chair with the big personality and marvelous lines is a hand-me-down from Suzie's mother-in-law. She reupholstered it with a hip chocolate brown zebra print from Brunschwig & Fils, giving it a sexy new look.

I am crazy about the textural mix of Suzie's sleek, glossy black coffee table sitting on a rugged java sea-grass rug. The striking curled shape of the table is the perfect counterpoint to the contemporary straight lines of the sofa. The seventies bamboo and cane chairs that she found on vacation in Chicago look swell when tossed into the mix, adding another natural color and texture. The one-of-a-kind Jonathan Adler caviar ceramic lamps add dramatic shine and texture. Glamorous pillows with a touch of metallic were fashioned from one of my favorite fabrics by Osborne & Little. (Were it legal to wed a textile, I'd gladly put a ring on it.) Other accent colors add pop and texture, like the tangerine silk and turquoise velvet pillows and an earthy clay African head Suzie found in a New Orleans junk shop. Suzie's design exemplifies the beauty found in fusing old with new, matte with sheen, and whimsy with high drama.

4
LIVE
YOUR
LIFE

Though one is more private and the other more public, both bedrooms and living rooms are meant for everyday life; therefore, make the decoration in these spaces a priority. Each room has distinct purposes that include relaxation, reflection, and communication, activities vital for enjoying life to the fullest. By all means, design and decorate both rooms for the way you really live; treat yourself as well as you treat any guest, and you will enjoy spending time in your home so much more. You only live once, so do it in style.

THE REAL DEAL

Your own bedroom should not be an afterthought but rather the first space for you to organize and decorate. Giving yourself a refuge from the world and being able to retreat to a restful, serene bedroom is one of the greatest luxuries you can enjoy. By the same token, the living room should not solely be a space to show off—it should be designed for the enjoyment of the people who actually live in the house (that includes kids, too). Having a room that is off-limits except for when you have company is archaic and devoid of what makes a home truly beautiful. It makes no sense to me to shortchange the room where you spend so much of your time—your bedroom—only to place all your energy and resources into a living room that you rarely use.

Having lived in a one-bedroom apartment for so long, I know the importance of maximizing the utility *and* beauty of my living room and bedroom. Firm decisions had to be made in order to create spaces

that were functional, super-comfortable, and still looked great enough to receive guests. It was an exercise in identifying what was truly necessary to live gracefully and figuring out how to incorporate those needs into a decorative plan.

Ironically, I learned this lesson early on from my summers at camp, where I stayed in a one-room cabin (oh, yes, my desire to beautify goes way back to Camp Chippewa on the crystal-clear Cass Lake in Minnesota). We had three sets of bunk beds with bright L.L. Bean wool blankets that also served as places to lounge. Trunks, decorated with colorful stickers, doubled as valuable storage and extra seating. A rustic painted table acted as a game table, a place to write letters, or the perfect spot for the occasional arm wrestle. Each boy was allotted his own small shelf displaying dear family photographs and objets d'art. On Sundays, I filled my canteen with cheerful wildflowers for the weekly inspection. Even in the small space and with my childhood budget constraints, everything a boy really needed for a bedroom and living room was there. When there is a comfortable place to gather, you go to bed laughing and talking and then sleep soundly under the stars. I have tried to replicate this peaceful and joyous spirit in every bedroom and living room since.

OVERLEAF *A Louis XIV chair covered in scarlet Fortuny, a Mario Villa Nefertitti coffee table, and an eighteenth-century Russian commode reign supreme with dazzling accessories in a regal yet relaxed living room.*

OPPOSITE *The warm butter-and-rose muted tones found in the antique Aubusson rug, the sofa, and the drapes define a welcoming feminine palette in this living room.*

An Hermès-inspired custom wall color, unrestricted light, gleaming polished floors, and sensational seating make this living room nothing short of divine.

BEDTIME STORIES

I used to believe that bedrooms are for two things only, one being sleep. But over time I have added to the list: primping, reading, rejuvenating, contemplating, and, most importantly, dreaming. When you really think about the amount of time you spend in your bedroom, and about how critical it is for your well-being to recharge, it becomes crystal clear that this room deserves your utmost attention and care. Many people save decorating their bedrooms for last, after ensuring that all the public spaces in the home are done and ready to be seen—or even worse, they never get around to it. I absolutely believe that the opposite is paramount: decorate your bedroom first with loving care. Only then, with your safe haven in place, should you turn your creative attention to all other rooms. In other words, put on your own oxygen mask first before assisting others. Create a special sanctuary all your own to nest and rest in, one that is soothing and calming to your spirit and easy on the eyes. This is definitely the time to pamper and indulge yourself, in a private space away from all the demands and pressures of the day, because if you don't, who will? Your bedroom is where you are the most intimate, where you are the most introspective, and where you dream. Design it to support and refresh your spirit and to be a room that nourishes your heart and soul

on a daily basis. By all means, pour yourself into a beautiful bedroom and enjoy it; you will thank me later.

SNOOZE HUES

In choosing a color palette for your personal retreat, think about what hues are harmonious and soothing to you. Colors that evoke relaxation and serenity, that trigger a deep emotional feeling of peace and safety, work best. In general, soft soothing tones—such as café au lait, crème, lavender, blush, sky, and celadon—are elegant choices for the bedroom. But for many people, dark milky chocolates and deep moody grays better signify comfort and protection than lighter tones. Give some thought to the colors that seem most heavenly to you. Engage these tones, and work forward from there. Guest rooms and children's rooms can certainly handle bold and vibrant color choices, as well as high contrast and wildly fun prints, but for me, a more meditative use of color and print is the way to go when creating a master bedroom that encourages lounging, catnapping, and dreamy slumber.

OPPOSITE *This Benjamin Moore wall color is aptly named Sweet Dreams. A complementary toile from Decorator's Walk for the drapes and a custom headboard accentuate the restful mood. A pair of white catalogue-chic side tables and Jonathan Adler ceramic lamps complete the dreamy look.*

THE MAIN EVENT

In any bedroom, the bed itself becomes the primary focal point; it can't be avoided. An attractive fireplace in the room or a large window with a super view is an added plus, but there is just no way around this simple design truth. With this in mind, as you establish the overall look of the room, think about how your bed can make the greatest design contribution possible. There are endless styles to consider, from the grandest to the most streamlined.

Selecting a bed style, like choosing a mattress, is deeply personal. All the variations of the tester, half tester, and canopied bed create a feeling of opulence reminiscent of eras past. Yards and yards of draped fabric cascading from under a gilt architectural remnant will often satisfy a princess or lord-of-the-manor tendency. Such treatments can also be just plain old fun. A little grandness never hurt anyone, so if you want to feel like a king or a queen, why not attach a carved crown above the bed with billowing panels of silk damask on either side, with ornate gold tiebacks? On the flip side, I love a highly glossed striated zebrawood bed in a classic angular deco style and graced with a gray cashmere coverlet and shams, but that's my inner Cary Grant talking. A sculpted headboard upholstered in a stunning fabric can immediately make for an impressive-looking bed. Think beyond the rectangle and camelback shape;

an exaggeration in proportion, such as a modified Chippendale pediment or a hint of chinoiserie pagoda, can definitely up the drama factor in the room. And don't forget nail heads; studs can be lots of fun.

What makes you comfortable is of paramount importance when choosing your bed. Don't feel like you have to stick to convention, and never sacrifice comfort for style when you can have both. For example, I am not a fan of footboards, so I always omit them. Some find their sleep nirvana on low, Zen-like Asian-inspired platforms, and some love the idea of being above it all. As they say, "Whatever gets you through the night, it's all right, all right."

Once you have settled on a style of bed you like, dress it to the nines with bedding that communicates the same design aesthetic. This is no place to skimp. Nothing is more seductive and sensuous than falling into a beautifully dressed bed. Sumptuous bedding, luxurious linens, ample soft pillows, and alluring tactile treats like angora blankets and faux-fur throws all serve to amplify the message: this is your place to close the door on the rest of the world, so you can indulge yourself in your own slice of heaven. The fabric used in a bedroom speaks volumes. Silky satins are just plain feminine and sexy in pale tones, evocative of a 1930s Hollywood starlet, while a rich pile of chocolate mohair velvet screams masculine. It's all a matter of your taste.

PEACE OUT

Addressing the bedroom windows is a must, as it is imperative to block out daylight, so that you can sleep well and in total darkness. I always choose flowing bedroom drapes that are solid, not printed, in wonderful natural fabrics such as silk, cotton, or linen; they feel relaxed and breathe life into the room. I shy away from window treatments that make me feel I must stand at attention. If the drapes are generous and give a sense of fluidity and ease, I am more restful.

Ambient lighting in the way of chandeliers and wall sconces create attractive romantic touches and add to the cozy atmosphere. Of course, bedside tables with large enough surfaces and drawers to hold necessities like a clock, a book, a glass, a decanter of water, and a good reading lamp are a must. A super-comfortable chair and ottoman or chaise is always a welcome addition for lounging and reading. A small desk for writing, a cozy carpet or rug to help buffer sound and to cushion your first steps as you start each day, and a mirror or two seem to be the only other functional ingredients really needed to satisfy the purposes of this room.

The bedroom is the perfect place to hang some of your most beloved personal photographs or works of art. I love nothing more than to lie in my bed, becoming totally lost in my thoughts as I gaze at pictures of family and friends that fill my heart

TIP If your life is on visual and emotional overload, one simple solution for creating a truly peaceful retreat is an all-white bedroom. No distractions—no color, patterns, clutter, or TV—just a cloud-like setting to allow complete calm and meditation. Creative dreaming can flourish more with a pure blank canvas as your palette.

with joy and gratitude, or to let endless minutes go by as I contemplate the beauty of my favorite paintings. I have specific accessories and decorative items in my bedroom, purposely well edited with one specific agenda in mind: making me feel happy. What is the last thing I want to see at the end of each day, and what makes me really smile when I first wake up? More importantly, what do I wish to share space with all those hours in between, during my most private, restful moments? Everything else is superfluous and distracting.

I know this will seem strikingly odd coming from an actor who makes his living on television, who grew up watching television, and who adores television, but televisions do not belong in bedrooms, no if, ands, or buts. I realize that we live in an era where all rooms, even bathrooms, are now outfitted with state-of-the-art media systems, and that a television in every room is a deluxe status symbol. But I must make a stand. Bedrooms are for slumber, meditation, nocturnal recreation, quiet conversation, and many other things—but not passive boob-tube viewing. The intrusion of the outside world is counter to the concept of creating a safe haven in your bedroom. Many people have stated that TV lulls them to sleep; years ago, many might have said the sound of the static "ant races" after the "Star-Spangled Banner," which played at sign-off, was soothing. But today, with hundreds of stations playing 24/7 and the never-ending bombardment of reality and news programs (and I use those words loosely), having a TV in the bedroom feels more like an invasion. Give peace and quiet a chance. Once you acclimate, you will be far more relaxed, creative, and satisfied if you forgo the telly in your bedroom.

On Stuff The bedroom is not the place to let stuff pile up or to pack in all the sentimental objects you can think of. They just become dust catchers. Clutter is an ever-growing, vicious little beast, and he doesn't know when to stop, so turn on your inner edit button and eliminate all the things in the room that are not needed. Then, carefully select a few key decorative accessories and watch how quickly a visual calm comes over the room.

TOP LEFT *An eighteenth-century painted and gilt door panel is an impressive headboard framed by yards of Scalamandré striped silk. Beefy chenille pillows and a faux fur throw complete this sensuous retreat.*

TOP RIGHT *When decorating with such a quirky color scheme for a traditional toile, it is best to truly commit. Manuel Canovas's Bengale in Paprika is used here with exuberant abandon.*

BOTTOM RIGHT *A crown-like architectural remnant from a Catholic church was discovered at Bush Antiques on Magazine Street and is an old-world canopy in this crisp blue and white guest room.*

BOTTOM LEFT *A soothing monochromatic palette and furnishings selected with refined restraint remind me of a sleek luxury liner stateroom. The straight lines of the fully upholstered bed and the handsome Biedermeier desk are masculine choices in this master bedroom.*

THE ROYAL TREATMENT

I f, like me, you have often wondered what happened to Cinderella post "happily ever after," well, here she is! Rest assured, three children later, she and her Prince Charming are doing just fine in this glamorous master bedroom. In a glance Melissa and Alfred Rufty's bedroom transports you to a sophisticated kingdom. The entire feel of the room is serene and calm, a romantic setting and a luxurious refuge, which is everything a bedroom should be. The furnishings and bedding, with dollops of gold throughout, are quite regal in nature, but because the room is spare, it never feels heavy-handed or cloying.

The walls are lacquered in Benjamin Moore's high-gloss enamel Milkshake Pink, the most seductive pink I have ever seen, with a perfect hint of cocoa to keep it from being too sweet. The rich, thick, and creamy paint color is restful and grown up, spelling out loud and clear "come lounge with me." The dreamy bed, with its gorgeous, ornately carved gilt headboard tufted with silk brocade, is raised to the heavens and dressed in exquisitely embroidered, appliquéd, and monogrammed silks. It's a pampering and indulgent treat-yourself-royally bed if ever there was one. I love the billowing wedding-gown bed skirt and the

simplicity of the luscious ivory drapes, both in Egyptian cotton. Beautiful Biedermeier bedside tables are kept free from clutter, and a cozy love seat is the only other furniture in this peaceful bedroom. Reading lamps, converted from a pair of charming porcelain vases found at Williamson Designs, and an oversized antique Italian carved gilt wood and iron chandelier complete the fairy tale in this perfectly romantic, elegant master bedroom.

Leslie and Bryan's Master Bedroom
NO PLACE LIKE HOME

One of the greatest gifts a home can give you is good bones— strong, solid construction, classic moldings, heart pine flooring, and a fluid floor plan are priceless. Such is the case with the home of my close friends Leslie Castay and Bryan Burkey.

After attending Tulane together, Leslie and I both hightailed it to New York City to pursue a career on the stage. For years we chased each other across Broadway, and even bought co-ops in the same neighborhood. But after marrying and starting a family, Leslie was drawn back to her roots, lured by a large home in New Orleans, nestled on a quiet tree-lined street with a yard for the children. She and Bryan found a beautiful corner Victorian just blocks away from where their daughters would attend school. Bryan is a talented artist and wine expert, and together they own WINO (Wine Institute of New Orleans), so when they learned that the home had a wine cellar, the deal was done. For decoration Leslie stuck to the basic rule of creating your own comfort zone first, which is even more important when you move across country with two girls under the age of five.

The master bedroom is situated on the second floor toward the rear of the home,

so that Mom and Dad can enjoy one of the house's many perks: a private balcony just perfect for a moment's escape or a place to unwind with a cocktail among the trees. For color Leslie drew from the wonderful views of both the western and northern skies visible from the floor-to-ceiling windows and chose the palest of soothing blues, Benjamin Moore Sea Foam. For the rest of the palette she drew inspiration from *Brown Sugar,* her husband's sensual painting that hangs proudly over the bed.

One of my favorite color combinations is brown and blue, and one of my favorite fabrics is my very own café au lait New Orleans toile that I designed for Hazelnut. Needless to say, I was very flattered when Leslie chose it for the bedding and the drapery. A pattern such as a toile or floral works best when it is used with edited restraint or excessive abandon—it's an all-or-nothing proposition. I'm glad she went with all. A Wedgwood blue-, brown-, and tan-striped tape with tailored rosettes is the perfect trim for the drape, which ties all the colors together. Texture plays a big part in the design of this space, especially with the headboard, which is Wedgwood blue tufted leather. On each side of the toile-draped king-sized bed are a pair of Oly mirrored nightstands with ample

storage, and atop are a pair of foo dog lamps from Hazelnut with chocolate brown silk shades.

Another accent color that Leslie chose is a beautiful shade of aqua, which is featured bedside on a Mario Villa plate and in a hexagonal garden stool that serves as an incidental table in the seating area. Leslie found a fantastic pair of mid-century modern chairs in her mother's attic and smartly sent them to her upholsterer for a faux cowhide fix. I love the little seating area near the fireplace—the silver leaf Louis Philippe mirror, the architectural spires, and especially the collection of Roseville vases in which she placed papyrus stems from her garden. But the magic ride in this room is the carpet from Nola Rugs; the color combination perfectly incorporates all the tones in Leslie's palette and serves as a grounding calm in the space.

Big, Easy Toile When Tom and I decided to open Hazelnut, we wanted to design something unique and signature for the shop. One day I caught myself staring at the Asian toile shower curtain in our New York bathroom, and I asked myself, "Why pagodas and bonsai? Why not historic French Quarter architecture and live oaks dripping with Spanish moss?" And my idea was born. I sketched images of the St. Louis Cathedral, the street car, the Natchez riverboat, and French Quarter scenes, and then I handed the drawings over to our talented friend and New York artist Sonia O'Mara Stuebe, who redrew the iconic images to perfection. I never imagined all the steps and ladders it would take to see this idea to fruition, but it was worth it. New Orleanians and lovers of the city have been taken with the fabric for years.

OPPOSITE *Atop the carved mantel sits a collection of celadon McCoy vases, which I gave to Leslie to celebrate her opening nights, and a lovely pencil drawing of her daughter, Audrey, which was a gift from the artist, Daniel Mark Duffy.*

LIVING ROOMS 101

As much as your bedroom is a private setting, rarely seen by guests, the living room is quite the opposite. It is a public space, to be used by all family members, and it is the primary place for entertaining guests. You will, of course, want your living room to have a "wow" factor. The space should reflect your good taste and be where you display some of your best art, collections, and furniture. But never make the room off-limits or for company only. Your living room should not feel like a dressed-up display in a wax museum, but rather a space where activities fill it with vitality and memories—the true standard by which to measure success in your décor. We all know those living rooms that feel like there hasn't been a laugh in them in years, and honestly, I can't wait to leave them, no matter how lavish they may be. Your living room represents your life, so it's essential to give it some soul.

Identify the activities that reflect the way you like to live, relax, and entertain, and then develop a design plan. You will gravitate to your living room more often if it is truly conducive to how you spend your downtime and if it relates to the type of gatherings you most enjoy. Do you like to sit by a crackling fire with a cozy book, lounge in front of a television watching old movies, or just sit quietly enjoying a

cocktail? When you entertain, do you envision a lively gathering, perhaps with a piano or place to play games, or will things be more centered around the art of a good conversation? Does your house also have a den or a family room, or is this one living room where all the gathering will take place? Once you have a handle on how you would like the room to function, everything about the decoration—the furniture plan, the fabrics, the accessories—should work toward creating a warm and inviting environment that says "you are always welcome here." Remember to think about luxury in terms of comfort and function, not in terms of how impressive the room can be. Everyone will want to spend more time in a living room that is user friendly, which really is the ultimate luxury.

WINDOW DRESSING

Many paint colors and window treatments work well in living rooms and can establish the mood you wish to create. This is a place where you can choose a bold color such as a deep red that makes a dramatic statement, or an elegant shade such as a pale teal blue

OPPOSITE *Nothing beats a crisp white oxford shirt paired with classic chinos. The same works in this unfussy, naturally relaxed living room. An ottoman upholstered in Clarence House tiger velvet fabric and a funky oversized vase by Julie Silvers add personal flair.*

that sets a more formal tone, or a sophisticated soft color such as fawn that is soothing. You can also go for more drama and impact in your window treatments in this room. You may love the opulence of big, billowy silk taffeta drapes puddling like a ball gown midcurtsy; soft, weighty wools, clean, straight, and trimmed with contrasting Greek key tape; or heavy yet classic Belgian linen simply hung from a classic iron return rod. This is a great opportunity to employ wonderful details like hardware, trim, tiebacks, patterns, and tassels, all of which add texture and visual stimulation. Whether you go with a formal or informal style, color and window treatments help set the stage for a room that you will love.

LAY IT OUT

The number-one ingredient that must work in any living room is the furniture plan. First and foremost, the furniture has to be attractive as well as comfortable. Nothing is worse than being short on comfort. So include an abundance of good seating—sofas, love seats, chairs, ottomans.

Most people place way too much importance on the sofa as the biggest decision in the room. I prefer the sofa to recede into the background, so that it's more of a support piece than the main attraction. This way, the attention stays on the art, fabric, interesting occasional tables, and the other seating in the room, which usually have far more personality. I am also not a

ABOVE *This fantastical chair is personality plus. Don't get stuck in a seating rut; think outside of the box like designer Melissa Rufty did when she scored this treasure on eBay.*

OPPOSITE *Attention to fine details makes a room, and I am crazy about the scalloped treatment on these lush silk drapes.*

huge fan of the supersized overstuffed sofas; comfort has its limits. At all costs, avoid overly stuffed sofas or fat chairs that resemble baseball gloves.

If your room has an obvious focal point like a fireplace, a piano, an engaging painting, or a window with an arresting view, you will want to arrange the seating around it. The driving factor for how to arrange your furniture, however, is a setup that encourages conversation. If your room is large, create more than one seating arrangement, so that everything is not lined up against the walls. It is impossible to really talk when furniture is too far apart; remember, it's not polite to yell across a room. Intimate spots for chatting and visiting or curling up with a book entice lingering and relaxation. Daybeds, chaise longues, and settees are interesting alternatives to the tried-and-true sofa or for a second seating area. They have so much personality and soul. And it is a great idea to have ottomans and stools tucked away here and there for extra seating at a party. Besides looking fantastic, these pieces of furniture are flexible enough to move around and accommodate the conversation flow of different occasions.

KEY ELEMENTS

The fabrics for upholstery should be just as welcoming and distinctive as the furniture you choose. Again, you will want the fabric to have a stylish and great look, but how it

feels is equally, if not more critical, to creating a cozy environment. Velvet is one of my favorite fabrics. It can hold the most saturated color imaginable, it feels heavenly, and it wears beautifully over time. I also love leather, flannel, suede, and tweed for living rooms; they are rich and elegant but not off-putting or too fragile. Silk is perfect for pillows and smaller chairs that perhaps may be used less often. A living room is the perfect place for strong colors, your favorite textiles, and patterns that add to the drama factor, like animal prints and bold geometrics.

Everything else you place in your living

room must contribute to the overall ambience you have established. Choosing unique coffee tables and side tables is a great way to bring in pizzazz and personality and, of course, for having a place to set down a drink and hold a lamp or two. Look for iron-based glass-topped tables, chunky Lucite tables, lacquered tables, or small Parsons tables. You can even refabricate an architectural fragment like a gate or door into a coffee table. I am head over heels about great little occasional tables that deviate from the norm. A marble-topped tripod twig table, a mainstay at Hazelnut, comes to mind, as well as any table by my pal Mario Villa. What I love most about these tables are their interesting legs, and I've always loved legs. They can be classic fluted Louis XVI or ornately carved ball and claw, but it's the oomph of the legs that gets me going. They create a great opportunity to really turn on the charm and rev up the *vavavavoom* factor that you really can't get with a sofa.

Depending on the type of flooring in the room, rugs can play a big part. There are two schools of thought when it comes to rugs. Some believe that a rug can be the focal point of the room, and its colors can be used to define the overall design scheme. I believe that the rug is part of the support system and should never be the entire focus, but rather it should complement the surroundings. After all, it's best to look upward to the stars or at least straight ahead—looking downward creates double

ABOVE *The warm, ruddy hues of a carved wooden Santos figurine, antique gilt crowns, and a vintage lamp from Lūm Vintage Lighting are enchanting elements against the cream sofa and Kravet drapes. And here is a trade secret: the sofa is covered in outdoor velvet from Perennials Fabrics, making it virtually child-, pet-, and Pinot Noir–proof.*

chins, and those are painful to remove. My favorite rug store is Nola Rugs, located down the block from Hazelnut. Their sophisticated selection has been edited to perfection; I have never seen a rug there that I didn't desire.

My tender spot when it comes to any room is the art. The marriage between decoration and art, the rare occasion when the two work seamlessly together, is nirvana. Your art must be personal. Avoid hanging a painting simply because it "goes well" in the room . . . that just screams *hotel,* not *home.* I understand acquiring art as an investment, but don't let that be the driving force behind the art you hang in your home. Otherwise, you might as well tack cold hard cash on the wall. Art should speak to you on a spiritual or emotional level; even if you cannot articulate why a certain piece moves you, go with your heart—it rarely lies. As in any other space, the accessories should be chosen judiciously; this is a room that by nature is prone to clutter—a *must* to avoid. Everything you own does not need to be shown. Think of it like those singers who oversing the national anthem, riffing out practically every note and making the melody virtually unrecognizable. Too much stuff in your living room will detract from the mood you are trying to create. Of course, throw a high note or two in the mix, but be true to your message, which is "welcome, relax, live a little."

ABOVE *A sleek cigarette table by metal sculptor Donald Tully is a modern accent in a traditional setting.*

OVERLEAF, RIGHT *I almost lose my head among these exquisite Louis XVI–period antiques. The graceful lines, polish, and patina are simply glorious. Pour me a drink while I pour myself into this sexy blue silk fauteuil.*

SHOW THOSE LEGS! Avoid using too many skirted pieces, which can feel weighted down and bottom heavy. Spring for furniture with legs. As a "gam" man myself, I realized long ago that unskirted furniture lets a room breathe, making it feel lighter and appear more open and graceful. So ditch those maxi skirts and put on a mini, or none at all!

The Robertses Living Room
EVERYDAY ELEGANCE

Caroline and André Robert's beaux arts mansion on Audubon Place rivals that of any Parisian boutique hotel in its grandeur and scale. The New Orleans house, built in 1906, is classical in design, with colossal paired columns greeting you as you enter the formal living room from the glorious front entrance. The bones of the space are outstanding: pristine architecture with stunning plasterwork, hardwood floors, and a white Carrara Marble mantelpiece, all original to the house. What could easily become a staid and overly formal living room, if decorated with a stuffy showplace point of view, is actually one of the most inviting and charming rooms in the entire house. Under the loving care of the beautiful and talented Caroline, this living room is infused with her unique and hip decorating vibe, creating a space that their family, which includes three children ranging from nineteen months to nineteen years, enjoys routinely. There is nothing imposing about Caroline's formal living room as she deftly mixes treasured family heirlooms and fine antiques with quirky vintage finds and contemporary pieces from Perch, her fabulous shop on Magazine Street. The fact that a toddler and two teenagers share this elegant and illustrious space makes me sit back and smile as I

ponder what the original owners might think about such a cool take on luxurious living.

The room is open and expansive with lots of natural light gracefully streaming in through the many floor-to-ceiling windows. Caroline adores all of the fresh colors of the wonderful parklike setting that surrounds the home, so she developed a custom color for the walls that she calls Perch Blue. It is one of the most delicious hues I have ever seen, a perfect blue-green-gray that is very close to Benjamin Moore's Colony Green. To highlight the magnificent details in the mill and plasterwork, all of the moldings and trim were painted in crisp Benjamin Moore's Decorators White. When Caroline could not find the exact shade of silk that she wanted for her window treatments, she had her workroom combine two different fabrics to create a striped coloration of watery blues and green. Yards and yards of this silk dress the windows, with traditional goblet pleats at the top and puddles of fabric at the hem tied back with gold-leafed acanthus leaves. The wall color, trim, and dressed windows set a perfect stage for Caroline's furnishings that is stately, fresh, and youthful.

The family loves to gather around the fireplace for conversation and relaxing, so Caroline arranged the furniture to

maximize the splendid carved mantel as the focal point. A large abstract expressionist painting by the Louisiana artist George Marks picks up on Caroline's favorite colors and lends a contemporary edge to the traditional fireplace. There is plenty of comfortable seating in a vibrant mix of color and style that further demonstrates Caroline's desire to keep things from getting too stodgy in her formal living room. She covered both her custom-designed comfy sofa and antique Louis XVI–style settee with durable, family-friendly velvet in citrusy lime green and chartreuse, and she anchored the seating area with an oversized glass and iron coffee table. I love the Hollywood feel of the Todd Hase silver-leaf rounded-back chair and the sleek contemporary feel of the iconic Philippe Starck ghost chair from Perch, which exemplify my belief that there is great personality in chairs and occasional seating that you can't easily replicate in a sofa.

The art, accessories, and accent furnishings in Caroline's living room are what give it that final "wow" factor and fully establish her goal of filling her living room with personal touches and family mementos rather than someone else's formula for opulence and formality. The silver-leaf altar torchères flanking her mantel are lucky finds from Magazine Street that she had made into lamps, and her mother gave her the porcelain statue of the goddess Shiva for Christmas many years ago. The

charming cloisoné clock and German porcelain oyster plate were handed down to Caroline from her parents and are subtle references to the stunning blue-green palette. A favorite vignette in the room is the handsome antique campaign secretary to the left of the fireplace that holds some of Caroline's most beloved treasures. She purchased the royal dux statue of the boy on the horse at auction, and the original foot sculpture, dated 1872, and the wonderful painting of a young girl are from an antiques dealer in Paris. Like Caroline, this living room is relaxed, chic, welcoming, and full of family history; it is the kind of room that first takes your breath away and then welcomes you in, inviting you to have an elegant glass of wine and enjoy great friendship and camaraderie in a stunning setting.

The Ruftys' Living Room
SOPHISTICATED CHARM

Melissa and Alfred Rufty entertain royally at home and are known for their glamorous cocktail and dinner parties, large and small. Their elegant living room adjacent to their formal dining room is decorated with a refined, urbane sensibility conducive to lively conversation and lingering over a delicious after-dinner drink. Everything about the room spells civilized entertaining, with its polished aesthetic and sophisticated design point of view. The glossy lacquered walls remind me of caramel fondant, and Melissa rightly calls it "drama in a can." Coat after coat of Benjamin Moore's Sepia Tan was applied with a brush after the walls were sanded as "smooth as a baby's behind," and a polyurethane top coat creates a glasslike finish. The look is high impact and sets the stage for the formality that Melissa is after.

An intriguing seating area is arranged near the fireplace that sits at the very end of the room. I love the sexy curved lines of the daybed from Uptowner Antiques upholstered in oyster silk and flanked by a fabulous pair of Adams chairs that Melissa inherited from her grandmother and re-covered in a high-energy rust Dedar Ikat. A brass inlaid French deco cocktail table from Jon Vaccari Design provides ample space

for setting down a cocktail while perusing an intriguing book or settling in near the fire for a good conversation. An eighteenth-century French trumeau placed above the painted mantel further enhances the gracious proportions of the room. I love the way Melissa surrounded the fireplace with two oil landscapes and a pair of eighteenth-century bronze sconces and hung it all lower than expected, making the seating group feel alluring and intimate.

What's great is that Melissa has managed to make the living room all about seating without making it all about the sofa. There is so much dynamic personality in this room, not only in the furniture selection but also in the well-edited collection of interesting accessories, that a guest would surely feel highly entertained just by taking it all in.

OPPOSITE *A bronze sculpture by Mary K. Morse from Cole Pratt Gallery dances with abandon in such delightful surroundings.*

5
THAT'S ENTER- TAINING

My father always said that I was a natural entertainer. I love being on stage, but enjoy entertaining at home just as much—it doesn't require memorizing lines, and I get to choose my own costumes. I adore the glamour of dining rooms and well-appointed bars, and I love to use these spaces, along with my kitchen, when having family and friends to my home. Designing these communal spaces in your home for sharing the good times in life should be a priority in any well-tended house.

NOW THAT'S "SWELLEGANT"

My impulse to entertain definitely harks back to my childhood, when, as a youngster, I would sneak into my parents' swanky cocktail parties. The ladies were always dressed to the nines in silk chiffon and taffeta dresses, while the gentlemen all wore ties with tie bars, cuff links, and often dinner jackets. There was a romanticism in that period: guests dressed the part. At many of these glamorous events, after saying good night to the guests at my bedtime, I would slip out of my room, procure an olive, and then make my way around the room dipping it in everyone's drink for a taste, until I was found out and whisked away. Once or twice among the din, I would sneak back undetected only to be discovered underneath the dining table in my Batman costume singing the refrain of Petula Clark's smash hit, "Downtown."

My parents' soirees seemed like the most fabulous of affairs, never pretentious, but fun and swell. There was always laughter and dancing; often my mother and Aunt Carol would break into a soft shoe if the moment was right. For the more formal events there would be a bartender and ladies passing hors d'oeuvres on silver trays, while a smart jazz trio roamed through the house. For less formal parties, Burt Bacharach would be spinning on the hi-fi while my dad played master mixologist behind the bar, which was his pride and joy. The construction of the bar was of his own mid-century design and incorporated a serpentine, high-gloss cypress base beneath a gleaming, copper countertop. The entire back wall was beveled mirror and outfitted with underlit glass shelving that housed interestingly shaped bottles and every colorful liquor known to man. Everything was picture perfect for the period. The size of my parents' budget for entertaining was irrelevant; it was the attitude and spirit that went into decorating their home for events that prevailed.

On the set of *Mad Men,* while wearing Janie Bryant's brilliantly designed costumes and living among Amy Wells's perfectly appointed sets, my childhood memories of my parents' oh-so-chic fetes came flooding back to me with vivid accuracy. Maybe we don't need all the smoking and boozy lunches, but I have never lost my fondness for a sexy cocktail and intimate dinner parties. And in addition to cocktail parties, a return to family and friends dining together at home—at a table, with cloth napkins, and without television—is an effort worth making.

OVERLEAF *Fabulous doors from Bush Antiques were the starting point for a grand bar and wine cellar.*

OPPOSITE *Photographs of Alfred Rufty's great grandfather making café brulot is a sentimental and stylish tribute to a beautifully stocked bar.*

LIFE'S A BANQUET

Dorothy Draper, the famed American decorator, once wrote, "Entertaining is fun!" I'd like to take that sentiment a step further. Entertaining *must* be fun; otherwise, what's the point? Entertaining should not be considered an obligation or chore; if it is, then it will feel the same to your guests. Sometimes the best soirees are impromptu and some of the most memorable are last-minute get-togethers with simple fare. Too much thinking leads to second-guessing, and second-guessing leads to panic . . . relax! It's just a party.

Keep the focus on what entertaining is really all about: the breaking of bread and sharing yourself and your home. Extending invitations and warmly welcoming people should be done only with great joy and the heartfelt desire to share camaraderie. Your home reflects your unique personality, and entertaining provides another opportunity to develop and share your signature style.

I love living in New York, New Orleans, and L.A., where there always seems to be a festive reason to gather. Whether a debutante ball or a crawfish boil, in New Orleans we celebrate life, death, and everything in between. Even at a christening or a funeral, there will be a party, complete with a full bar and a lavish spread. In New York and Los Angeles, I've attended opening-night parties for Broadway and glamorous award events; a highlight was the after-party for the Screen Actors Guild awards. In an over-the-top setting, the designers managed to create intimate lounge areas where we celebrated and hobnobbed. But my favorite type of party, above all, is the self-catered dinner party at home. Preparing the house, setting the table, planning the dinner, and, of course, all aspects of the décor come into play. Besides, no one ever asks, "Who are you wearing?"

DINNER WITH NO RESERVATIONS

It seems like what has been lost in the shuffle of our hectic lives is the beauty of a simple dinner party. Time has given way to a more casual form of entertaining, which has its place and time, but for me, there is nothing lovelier than an intimate dinner party.

As a child, I loved watching my mother prepare and attend to all the details for an elaborate buffet or a seated dinner. In college, my brother and I would borrow our parents' home to throw our own dinner parties. His were called "New Talent Night," where the mandatory rule was that each invited guest bring a date that no one else had ever met. Mine were alfresco dinners for up to sixteen friends on the patio. I'd push all available tables together

OPPOSITE *A simple farm table, heirloom china arranged around a chinoiserie mirror, and whimsical felt garland strewn through a chandelier send a warm and festive invitation to dinner.*

underneath the large awning, cover them with white linen, and then go to town arranging potted geraniums and tall hurricane lamps down the center of the long makeshift table. I had no idea how to cook, but I was determined to do it all myself, so I made sure the recipes were easy and obviously foolproof. Although this kind of dinner party may have been a little formal for some college students, my crowd dined and danced all night.

Signature Cocktail At every party, we always serve one signature drink. Guests love trying something new and unexpected. It was fun to name a drink, the Tequila Mockingbird II, which is on the menu at Commander's Palace and is also featured in the book *In the Land of Cocktails* by Ti Martin and Lally Brennan. Here is the recipe.

TEQUILA MOCKINGBIRD II *Makes one drink*

2 ounces tequila
1 ounce Limoncello
1 ounce lemon juice
2 drops Angostura bitters
½ ounce simple syrup

Combine all ingredients in a cocktail shaker full of ice. Shake well, and strain into a martini glass.

I JUST ADORE A PENTHOUSE VIEW, HOWEVER . . .

Never let a small apartment or house limit your entertaining—square footage never inhibited my desire to throw a party. The true spirit of entertaining should not be defined by anything but your imagination and sense of style. New York (or any big city) is actually a great training ground and a laboratory for cultivating wildly clever ideas and unleashing design creativity. Not only is there a barrage of constant inspiration from the talent the city attracts, but everything you need is always just a few blocks away. The flower district is an amazing treat for the senses and easy for procuring blossoms, from the most exotic to the ordinary. A trip to Chinatown yields strings of lights with Japanese lanterns to hang overhead, and a call to the neighborhood sushi joint for delivery makes for a great gathering at a moment's notice. New Yorkers are known for having black-tie parties in one-bedroom apartments and cookouts on the roof. For many events, my friends and I would move half of the furniture to the basement to make room for a dance floor, put coatracks in the hall, and ice the champagne and wine in the bathtub.

Being clever with what you have is the key. One important lesson I learned from living in New York is that there is absolutely no reason to wait for more space, more money, or more of anything to enjoy one of life's most rewarding pleasures: entertaining.

TAKE YOUR SEAT

In general, dining rooms are not used nearly as much as they should be. I am not a fan of the dining room that is visited only at Thanksgiving. The dining room should be well thought out and designed so that your family and friends can enjoy it happily and often. It's great to be able to really use this space on an everyday basis, making it the focus of the evening meal, as well as special occasions. So no texting, no TV, no cell phones—let's enjoy the lost art of conversation.

THE MAIN COURSE

The size of your dining room will determine the size and shape of your table. As much as the traditional rectangle and oval are classics, there is something outstanding about a round table. All King Arthur references aside, I love the fact that there is no head of the table and conversation can flow like the unity of the circular shape itself. Banquettes can offer a stylish solution for more narrow dining spaces or a corner dining nook. They can give an intimate, romantic feel reminiscent of a Parisian bistro, or depending on your own twist, they can be streamlined with the flair of a mid-century diner.

Though they may seem outdated, break-fronts and buffets were designed for a good reason. Your china and crystal can be displayed beautifully until it is time to be

ABOVE *An Oly shell chandelier, simple slipcovered chairs, and a painted server spell intimacy in a small dining space*

OPPOSITE *An over-the-top mirror, a hand-marbled gilt ceiling, and Schumacher's Brighton Damask grass cloth set the stage for drop-dead drama.*

used, and a server to store your linens and silver can double as a splendid surface for candlesticks, urns, lanterns, or other decorative objects that you love. You can keep the look from becoming too staid by placing artful or playful objects in both, further defining your style and personality, and changing out the accessories to reflect the seasons.

Often it can be a challenge to select dining chairs that are both elegant and comfortable, but if a man can be put on the moon, the perfect chair for your needs can be found. If your chairs are a bit formal and rigid, they will help with our ever-declining good posture, and, in reality, we don't sit all night at the table. Be careful, though, of fragile antique chairs: as much as I love the beauty of period dining chairs, but most are just too frail for use. (Nothing is more embarrassing for a guest than to be

ABOVE *A cool lemon and lime color palette in the drapery, accessories, and a painting by Nicole Charbonnet keep this dining room crisp, clean, and contemporary. Benjamin Moore's wall color in Cape May Cobblestone allows the zesty colors to pop.*

OPPOSITE *The exuberant use of tangerine and the embroidered border on the drapes keep this dining room whimsical and fresh. An intricately carved seventeenth-century Swedish dining table from Somat House Antiques and simple French chairs live cheerfully beneath the ethereal metal chandelier by Paul Gruer.*

told not to sit in a certain chair; it's even worse if a chair actually collapses.) Dining chairs must be sturdy and completely functional if you intend on using your dining room—save weight distribution for airline travel.

Your chairs can greatly contribute to your dining room's look. Mix it up by trying tall wingback host and hostess chairs upholstered in a contrasting color or pattern to the rest of the dining chairs. Or collect chairs of various styles and lacquer them all in the same fabulous color.

If your home or small apartment does not have a designated dining room or area due to lack of space, don't let that stop you from having dinner parties. Use your imagination. Clear off a desktop and drape it with a tablecloth. For additional seating, look to stools and benches or stylish folding chairs that easily tuck away in a closet. I love the clear acrylic ones we carry at

---

Dimmers and Candlelight As I learned in theater, always be aware of lighting in a space. No one looks good in fluorescent or energy-efficient lighting, especially as we grow older . . . so dim all the lights, sweet darling. Put every lamp or chandelier on a dimmer, and use candlelight to create a warm, welcoming mood. Repeat after me: use dimmers and light candles. You'll thank me later: it's simple, it's easy, and it's far less expensive than plastic surgery.

Hazelnut; they are virtually transparent so they blend perfectly with any style without taking up any "visual space" in a room.

IN THE MOOD

Lighting in a dining room, like in every room, should be given top priority. You want to be able to see your food and your guests, but also create a romantic glow. Remember, this is not a cafeteria. A striking overhead fixture, such as a crystal chandelier, adds just the right amount of drama to your room, supplying plenty of sparkle and light. Hang the fixture as low as possible over your table and bask in its beauty. I also appreciate the wonders of candlelight and while it may not be practical to have your chandelier outfitted for candles, sconces or a candelabra offer the perfect opportunity to use wax. Even a simple pair of candlesticks or several votives arranged on the table casts enchanting light. Creating the best mix of natural and artificial lighting in the dining room can be achieved only by trial and error and by manipulating all the components.

OPPOSITE *This masculine dining room is all about modern shapes, strong lines, and natural elements. An oval table by Glenn Armand and a handpainted striped vintage buffet are sleek counterpoints to the organic free-form chandelier from Gerrie Bremermann Design.*

THIS GUY WALKS INTO A BAR . . .

I worship adult libation stations. There is nothing more captivating and seductive than a sparkling bar, set up and stocked with crystal and trays and all the barware accessories that gleam like jewelry. Displaying your decanters, martini shakers, and accoutrements is a lovely way to add significant beauty to your home while serving a very important function: the cocktail hour.

What I truly love about an imaginative bar is that it can be achieved in any home on any scale. A well-tended and decorated bar can be any size, and it does not have to cost a fortune. Some of the best bars I have ever seen are created in a tiny space cleverly carved out in a room—on a console or tucked away in an attractive cabinet. Choosing to make the space for a bar sends a strong message to guests that adults reside here and that elegant relaxation matters. Of course, I have seen my share of sensational bars, as well as whole rooms designed to meet this need and entire pieces of furniture turned over to this higher power. More spacious spots for serving and enjoying cocktails, complete with cushy seating that says loud and clear, "Belly up," are a nice addition to any design scheme. I love the combination of a library and bar, and especially crave a cozy spot where I can listen to music while sipping a glass of wine. The bottom line is you can take your

bar as far as you wish. But really all you need are a few striking decanters, your favorite glassware, and a dedicated space in which they can reside.

ABOVE *Simply set atop a rouge marbled eighteenth-century console, gleaming decanters and cognac seduce the senses.*

OPPOSITE *This "Marrakesh Express" bar explodes with dynamic color. The walls, upholstered in Alhambra by Pierre Frey, set the tone for a festive cocktail hour.*

ABSINTHE MAKES MY BAR GROW FONDER

The bar in our new home is a dream come true. I adore both eighteenth-century French antiques and a well-designed bar, and the fact that the previous owners did, too, was kismet. A master carpenter converted a stunning walnut armoire into a wet bar and outfited the interior with custom cabinetry, refrigerator, and ice maker. The thick soapstone counter holds a seventeenth-century Chinese ceramic bowl converted into a small sink. The wonderful thing about housing your bar in a beautiful piece of furniture is that when you want it to go away (but, really why would you?), just close the doors. I leave the doors open all the time to gaze upon the collection of barware I've accumulated over the years.

A focal point of our beautiful bar is a gorgeous antique gilt mirror that our dear friend Katy gave us for Christmas. She found it in the Paris flea market and knew it was right up my mirrored alley. Tom hung it in the center of the bar, and its crackled glass shimmers as it reflects the sparkle of the crystal and silver. For a bit of whimsy and artistic effect he placed a pair of Mariovilla tin palm fronds peering from behind the mirrors. I stacked my collection of decanters and bottles on an ornate silver tray that was given to my parents as a wedding gift, and then layered in my grandfather's antique sterling martini shaker and the Baccarat crystal double old-fashioneds that Tom and I carried back from our first trip together to Paris. Gold-striped 1940s glassware found at RetroActive and 1960s Steuben teardrop stemware round out my collection of vintage barware. Everything comes together to create a dazzling bar that is uniquely ours.

Olive or Twist No matter how large or small your bar, stock it with the right accessories:

- Ice bucket (of course).

- Waiter's corkscrew—learn how to use one.

- Cocktail shaker—opt for stainless steel.

- Jigger—until you can eyeball measurements.

- Juicer—choose a wooden reamer or "dish" with a spout for easy pouring.

- Strainer—to keep that pesky ice out of your "up" drinks.

- Bar spoon—for stirring when shaking is a no-no.

- Muddler—well, for muddling.

- Proper glassware—look for glasses of appropriate size that make a lady look like Audrey and a gentleman look like James Bond.

- Linen cocktail napkins—because we are grown-ups now.

SOMEONE'S IN THE KITCHEN

It's inevitable that at any function in your home, people will gather in the kitchen. Don't fight it. Without hiring proper security, they will come, so you might as well embrace it. Foodies and people who love to cook enjoy sharing their passion and don't want to be isolated and disassociated from the gathering. For them a kitchen is more than a place to sling hash; it is a communal area where experimentation and conversation abound. Family and guests are always supremely curious about what is going on in the kitchen, unable to resist taking a peek or even wanting to help. Your kitchen should not be considered "backstage" and off-limits; rather, it can take center stage and will often entertain tremendously.

My favorite kitchens are those that have well-functioning workstations where the chef can get the job done, with a spot for "helpers" to pull up a stool to watch and even be assigned a task. With such a setup, conversation can flow easily, and often the crowd will expand. I can't help but get a warm, easy feeling when I think about the basic function of this space—the preparation for the nourishment of loved ones. So make your kitchen as appealing and inviting as possible.

The kitchen is the heart of a home. It is used by every member of the family, and depending on your brood it can be a space where so many other activities besides cooking and eating occur. Innately, it is a gathering place where life is shared—in other words, it is home base. The flow of a kitchen is most important, and for each household the needs will be slightly different. If you are at all confused about what layout works best for you, keep a running journal or list of how often and to what extent you use your kitchen. Will you require a lot of counter and work space? Will you snack in the kitchen at counter stools, or will most family meals be served at a table? Are you tight on space where every inch counts, or is this a big, open dream kitchen? Will this room also be used for homework and computer time? A specialist can help with suggestions, but only you know how you and your family will inhabit the space.

Don't fall into the trap of cluttering your kitchen with every newfangled, high-tech, and never-used specialty appliance. These status symbol extravagances, when not utilized, tend to make the owner appear foolish and wasteful. However, if you are a

OPPOSITE *A formal crystal chandelier pairs beautifully with humble subway tile in a grand but grounded kitchen. Who says you can't have dramatic lighting when you're cooking? The crisp, glossy all-white look is punctuated with robin's egg blue vintage Le Creuset cookware and the chandelier's simple paper shades painted by the homeowner.*

ABOVE *A collection of country French pottery and copperware exudes maximum charm in this snug French Quarter space.*

RIGHT *Minimal, modern, and chic defines this sleek, streamlined kitchen.*

Setting Up the Kitchen When arranging a kitchen, I recommend thinking like an actor. Set the stage so that while you prepare and cook, your supporting cast and audience will see your face and not your back. Be a star for a moment or two. The kitchen is a hub, and everyone will come in at some point, so create easy spaces where guests can pull up a chair or stool or even just lean up against a counter to converse or join in. This must be a working set, so if you choose to display your pots, make sure you can reach them, unless they are too old and must be used solely as wall hangings, such as antique molds and turn-of-the-century culinary accoutrement.

gourmet and love to make your own pasta, bread, ice cream, gelato, sausage, and wine . . . go to town! Otherwise, a simple KitchenAid mixer will suffice, and use classic stainless steel or fun enamel cookware colors to your advantage. For years, Tom has collected cherry red Le Creuset cookware, known for its high performance and classic style. Not only does he use these colorful pots daily, they also earn their design keep when off duty. Be sure to designate a convenient place for the things you continually reach for, so they are handy and make maximum use of available space.

The art in your kitchen can range from the latest school projects created by a second-grade Matisse to the most formal still life. The kitchen is a wonderful place to enjoy art. Some may feel that the appropriate art should be country or primitive in feel, but I believe that the art in your kitchen should reflect the same taste that you employ throughout your home. It can, of course, be more playful or colorful, but give it the same importance that you do any other room.

LEFT *Have fun with simple displays. Here, life imitates art (and vice versa).*

OPPOSITE *This sun-drenched breakfast room nestled within the kitchen is cheerful with its country French farm table, Italian wood-beaded antique chandelier, and high-backed chairs slipcovered in Brunschwig and Fils Avignon fabric.*

I CAN SEE CLEARLY NOW

One word to describe Caroline and André Robert's breakfast room is "breathtaking." The entire space embodies her design philosophy of bringing the outdoors inside, and it's done with a wonderfully easy style and panache. It's no wonder that this space is one of her favorites in her home—it is nestled close to the kitchen and family room and is situated alongside a bank of floor-to-ceiling glass French doors that open to a lush green garden, gorgeous antique fountain, and patio. Serving brunch has never been more inspiring.

In keeping with the natural indoor/outdoor vibe, Caroline covered the walls in a textural grasscloth by Roos International. The floor throughout the area is sealed polished brick laid in a classic herringbone pattern. Billowing from floor to ceiling are silk bluebell draperies with snazzy pinch pleats masterfully designed by Perch's Jack Mayberry. They hang from a simple, antiqued iron self-returning rod, which creates a nonfussy appeal.

The centerpiece of the room is the round zinc-covered antique table from Perch that allows for ample seating as well as easy communication, whether at breakfast, lunch, or dinner . . . or in our case, with a freshly baked batch of lemon cookies and cold iced tea, lovingly prepared by Caroline's mother. Perch has many wonderful chairs. I'm sure it was a tough decision, but I love that Caroline chose Lucite ballroom chairs covered in Trina Turk's festive and colorful Super Paradise print for Schumacher. The bold geometric pattern in turquoise, citron, and marine is both retro and modern, injecting a breezy high-fashion feel that is true to Caroline's style. The chairs' transparency really captures the bright rays of the sun pouring into the room and makes the entire space sparkle with life. The table is set with a vintage Wedgwood pattern that reflects the lovely tones of the space, and, saving some fun for later, Caroline continues to collect pieces from estate sales and auctions. She and I share the love of mixing silver: I mix my grandmother's antique pattern with the classic Tiffany Shell and Thread, while Caroline mixes Reed & Barton's Burgundy and Francis I. The whimsical "frog on lily pad" salt and pepper shakers are a favorite at Hazelnut, and the choice of Saint Louis Bubbles crystal accompanied with a blanc de chine statue from an estate sale perfect the mix. The oversized gilt Italian chandelier adds a sense of grandeur that never overpowers the room. There is such a welcoming feel to this space that one cannot resist pulling up a chair—the exact mood a dining space should evoke.

6
GREAT THINGS COME IN SMALL PACKAGES

Remember all the fun you had decorating your dorm room? Well, the fun does not have to stop there. Having lived in small apartments for more than half of my life, I've come to relish facing the challenges of making them function well and look great. Although the size of the room may be restricted, your imagination and sense of style isn't. Think outside of the box and about the inside of *I Dream of Jeannie*'s bottle: no living space could have been smaller, but it was beyond fabulous.

EQUAL OPPORTUNITY DESIGN

Even large homes have a small space or two, which should not be treated as an afterthought. They deserve the same design respect and attention that you give the grander rooms in the house. There are indeed some inherent limitations when dealing with pocket-sized spaces—so maybe a billiard table will not fit in your studio apartment. But because of the reduced square footage, this is often the place to get the most bang for your buck. Perhaps you can use that pricey wallpaper that you have been eyeing or expensive tile you covet. One fabulous painting or sensational mirror is often all that is needed to establish a significant impact. Try featuring a bold geometric pattern that draws from the color palette of the other rooms or employing that opulent wallpaper that you really love but couldn't envision covering larger walls. A small space, thought-fully considered, can actually reward you with a big design payoff, if you only think small in scale and not in personality and potential.

SUPPORTING CHARACTERS

When pressed for space, the critical first step is to think about what your needs are for the room and how it should function. If there are problems to solve, tackle them early on. Do you require more storage, shelving, and places to stash real-life loot? Do you need a seating plan or is this a room that requires work surfaces, like a desk? Taking a fresh look at your space will allow you to design it to operate well for the true tasks at hand, or to multitask if need be. It is imperative to be certain that a small room, first and foremost, serves its true purpose. There is no space to waste, and function should always come first.

The next step is to edit, which may sound disingenuous coming from an avid collector like myself, but editing, essential in all rooms, is absolutely mandatory when decorating compact spaces. We all tend to accumulate too much stuff that we really don't need and may never use. But storing, organizing, and otherwise hiding all of it can get pretty unwieldy, and clutter is not your friend, especially in small spaces. Focus your attention on what you really want to make the cut. Sentiment is fine, but don't let that be the driving force behind every decision. Everything in the room

OPPOSITE *This tiny home office packs big style in an artist's cottage. The corner is outfitted with an ebony and ivory inlaid desk. A full-length mirror enlarges the space.*

OVERLEAF *In a narrow hall in this cottage, a sleek faux patent leather banquette sits opposite a flatscreen TV. Style abounds in this small but high-functioning space covered in Rouge Manual Canovas Nantes wallpaper.*

Make the Most of It Here are other strategies to increase visual comfort in tight places:

- Paint low ceilings a light color with a glossy finish or even a metallic to reflect light.

- Keep all trim and moldings the same as the wall color to keep the eye moving throughout the room.

- Forgo a chandelier or overhead light fixture in favor of floor or table lamps and wall sconces. A fixture hanging from the ceiling can weigh the room down.

- Let the sunshine in! Keep the window treatments as unfussy as possible. Bare, uncluttered windows, especially if the view is nice, are your greatest asset for creating a sense of space; use simple shades if privacy is needed.

- Hang drapery as high as possible, mounted as close to the ceiling as you can to draw your eye upward.

- For walls, rugs, and fabrics, limit your palette to two colors with a third accent hue for an ordered, harmonious feeling throughout the room.

must pull its own weight, either increasing efficiency or adding to your design message. Donate any piece of furniture that you are not really using, and remove any object that does not pass the "love" test.

After you've pared down the clutter and organized the room, define your point of view. A petite room can pack an enormous decorative punch, if it is carefully planned and designed with full commitment. First, consider color. Whether you go light or dark, in choosing a palette, you'll give your small room panache. Light colors can sometimes make a room feel larger, but used alone, they are not enough to trick the eye completely. You'll also need to factor in other elements to create a truly heightened sense of scale and space. With that in mind, don't feel like you have to give some of your favorite and more saturated hues the cold shoulder. Some of my favorite little rooms make use of sensationally bold choices in color, either on the walls or furniture. A strong and effective color statement will draw attention to mood and personality in the room rather than size. Small rooms merit colors that tell the world (just like the smallest Who in Whoville), "We are here, we are here, we are here!"

OPPOSITE *Even in tight quarters you can find an imaginative way to display your pretties and hide your not-so.*

THINK BIG

In a small space, nothing goes unnoticed. With this in mind, aim for the best quality you can in your furnishings and fabrics, and remember that everything must be there for good reason—and don't think small. Your home may be as petite as a dollhouse, but don't decorate it with dollhouse furniture; doing so will only reinforce the preexisting message. A large-scale piece of art or a grand armoire can actually trick the mind's eye. Of course, you can't stuff the room like a sausage with lots of bulky furniture, but one or two significant pieces will improve the function of the room and make a bold visual impact. A nice-sized sofa, for example, can satisfy seating needs and look decidedly important, and a tall bookcase adds the illusion of height while meeting storage needs.

A mirror is one of the most satisfying elements you can give a small space, so give generously. Place a mirror on a wall that opens up to another room, and you'll double your visual square footage.

Just because a room is undersized does not mean it must be underserved. One strong print and a texture or two can punch up the volume and give definition without taking up space. Rugs should be as large as possible, so don't think postage stamp.

ABOVE *A cozy reading nook is carved out of a small space beneath a window's great architectural detail.*

OPPOSITE *Take a closer look at the square footage beneath your stairs or atop your landings and envision a sensuous hideaway or spot to bask in all day.*

TIP When coming up with a scheme for a room that you'll see every day, avoid creating décor that's overly themed, especially in a small space where the message can be taken too far too easily. Leave themes to reality decorating shows that require time limits and shock value. So you are interested in astronomy—read a book, but don't paint the heavens on your bedroom ceiling and hang a portrait of Galileo above a four-poster bed made of telescopes. It's not real, and you'll quickly tire of it. (And one day, you may be interested in zoology, so what then?)

Kathleen Allain's Attic Bedroom
TRIP TO THE BEACH

ABOVE *A mellow yellow Chippendale-style chair is a zippy accent color pulled from the Pontchartrain Beach fabric.*

OPPOSITE *A collection of style books alongside a whimsical gouache painting by Marc Foster Grant, which features a girl's best friend, satisfies the inner fashionista.*

NEXT PAGE *Cheerful and spirited accessories like painted tole pagoda tealight holders, a kiwi-colored gourd-shaped lamp, and a ceramic dove vase are youthful touches in a room that spells "fun."*

The natural step after designing the New Orleans toile was to create a completely different fabric that celebrated not only New Orleans, but also the entire Gulf Coast region. So, for our second signature fabric, I chose exuberant shades of lemon, hot pink, kelly green, and turquoise that evoke summer with pop art–inspired icons of palm fronds, crowns, hand-drawn fleur-de-lis, and even crustaceans, all arranged in a patchwork pattern reminicent of vintage Palm Beach. I named it Pontchartrain Beach, after the beloved deco beachside amusement park that my grandfather built in the twenties.

The happy fabric simply makes me smile, and I was pleased to hear that it did the same for artist Suzie Allain's daughter. When the family moved into a charming hundred-year-old uptown New Orleans cottage, Kathleen opted for the converted attic bedroom. Although the ceiling is low, the small room gets a great deal of light, but the funky shaped space with its slanted back walls proved a décor challenge.

Kathleen is a vibrant teen with a flair for art and fashion who uses her room for everything from homework and projects to, of course, hanging out with friends. She and her mom chose to use the colorful Hazelnut's Pontchartrain Beach as the star of the room, and in a big way. With yards

and yards of the cheerful pattern creating a tentlike feel in the small alcove, this room seems to say, "I may be small, but I am not boring!"

When dealing with an odd-shaped room, especially a small one, if you choose a color or pattern, go with it. There can be no fence-sitting. By employing one definitive pattern all over rather than mixing several, Suzie and Kathleen actually unified the space, bringing every corner together.

The vintage bed was in desperate need of a refurbishing coat of paint, but instead of using the obvious whitewash, a fun fuschia was pulled from the fabric, creating a strong focal point for the space. On either side of the bed, matching white tables were added, both for function and to tie in the white walls of the room. This adorable vignette sits on a yellow- and white-striped dhurrie rug bought from Nola Rugs on Magazine Street.

An installed window seat features a mélange of whimsical pillows from Hazelnut, Anthropologie, and Target on top of a long cushion that doubles as a twin bed for sleepovers. Colorful ceramic garden stools are placed throughout the room for additional seating and writing surfaces. A white plank desk serves as a study space, project center—and, of course, a makeup and beauty station. My favorite stylish additions are the green ceramic lamp, the vintage carousel letter, and the light-up cherry blossoms, all from Hazelnut. Next to the desk is an entire framed cork wall covered in the Pontchartrain Beach fabric, giving maximum space for posting inspirational photos, postcards, and pictures of pals and family.

THE LUXURIOUS LOO

A great opportunity to create drama and go for broke in a small space is with your powder room. You won't spend a great deal of time here, so make every moment count. Powder rooms are diminutive, often tucked away in a hall or hidden under a stairwell, so think of this room as a perfect chance to express yourself and get your ya-yas out. Go with something truly whimsical or something slightly over the top, just be sure to focus in on the details as you create candy for the eye in this tiny space. Perhaps take your guests on a trip somewhere exotic when they visit your powder room—be inspired by *The Last Emperor, Out of Africa,* or *The Secret Garden.* Anything goes in this room, so whatever story you tell, tell it with panache. Anyone can slap on some paint, hang a ring or two, and display a pair of pretty guest towels, but we are not just anyone.

You may choose to start with one great detail and fly with it: add to the mix a sensational tile, fascinating marbles, terrazzos, or alabasters; consider mixing them in interesting graphic patterns. As for the walls, no color is too saturated or pattern too complex. But don't stop there: a fabulous vessel sink and outstanding hardware help raise the design bar. Try an oversized chandelier in a different, unexpected color, artistically sculptured faucets, or a recycled antique bowl converted into a basin. If you've got a sense of humor, use it: one of my favorite small bathrooms features an antique altar candlestick fashioned into a toilet paper dispenser, which was a tongue-in-cheek way to decorate the guest bath. Always remember this isn't your everyday bathroom, so take risks that you may not take elsewhere in the home.

ABOVE *Rethinking the use of an alter candlestick gives all new meaning to the word throne.*

OPPOSITE *Summer Palace wallpaper by Osbourne and Little is the singular sensation in this luxe Asian-inspired powder room. All other details follow suit.*

MAKE AN ENTRANCE

Your entranceway should be much more than a place where you drop your keys or kick off your shoes. I believe in immediate gratification, and it is paramount to set the stage from the get-go. Embrace the power of first impressions and acknowledge the fact that whether your foyer is petite or grand, you have only a limited amount of square footage to make that first impression.

When I think foyer, I can't help but visualize Aunt Mame descending her spiral staircase at her ever-glamorous Beekman Place flat. That emotional impact, achieved in your own way, is what you should strive for in your foyer. You want your visitors to feel welcome and at home, and you may also be aiming to wow and impress. Either way, you should create a specific mood for this space. Whether your home is a mansion with a formal marbled foyer and a grand spiral staircase, a blinding crystal chandelier, and portraiture worthy of a Vanderbilt, or a simple, cozy cottage with a classic gilded mirror above a console in the entryway, clearly define your personal style. Your foyer should be inviting and compelling, as it will hint to your guests what is yet to come.

My grandfather Harry Batt was a tall, strapping gentleman with great style, flash, and showmanship. When he walked into a room, you knew there was something special about him. On his arm was my grandmother, ever stylish yet far more subtle and subdued, making a completely different statement. Upon entering their strictly deco foyer, which was unique for a New Orleans home, guests were greeted by a crescent-shaped staircase built from cypress and Lucite that climbed along a side wall composed entirely of floor-to-ceiling glass blocks. Guests instantly knew they were in for something special, unique, and wonderful: the company of my grand-parents. It is important to have a clear vision of how you want people to feel when they enter your home, and more importantly, how *you* want to feel when you arrive.

If the traditional and often necessary "last-look mirror" is not your taste for your entryway, you'll find endless possibilities for creating such a focal point. An engaging work of art can help to set the scene, or a collection of items prominently displayed on the wall, as long as you want it to be what greets you every day.

While helping my brother and sister-in-law decorate the foyer of their new home, we used antique painted friezes, panels, and various architectural fragments found at auction and hung them together

OPPOSITE *Hindoustan Zuber panoramic murals lend immediate gravitas to a French Quarter entranceway, beckoning you on an exotic and romantic journey.*

along the tall walls, forming an impressive collection that added a sense of gracious age and romantic grandeur. This is a wonderful example of how something unexpected for your foyer or entryway can make a great impression.

A SAVVY SOLUTION

An elegant wall treatment for your foyer can be achieved without costing a fortune. If a certain wallpaper you love is not in your budget, paint and the use of color is a more affordable option and can create similar effects. During my early years on Broadway, I would often find myself spending a great deal of my free time at the Decoration & Design Building on Third Avenue, where I would play "Bryan's dream house," pawing the fabrics and drooling over the furniture. At one showroom, I discovered a gorgeous wallpaper that was made of actual gold leaf, and I could instantly see it gracing the walls of my tiny foyer. However, it was simply not in my budget, even if I did the old mac-and-cheese routine for a few months. Try as I might, I couldn't get the image out of my mind and knew it was the only way to go for that space. No other solutions

could compare to the gold leaf wallpaper of my dreams.

After a few weeks I made a fortuitous visit to SoHo. While strolling through the art galleries as I regularly did between shows, I came across the Arthur Roger Gallery. My eyes were immediately drawn to the backdrop walls of the fantastic photography show. Although the images were dazzling, it was the walls that captivated me. Arthur told me they had used gold metallic enamel paint to create the gilded effect, and he kindly gave me the paint name, Antique Gold Enamel. I found it at Pearl Paints, rushed home and went to town on my walls. The results were not only fantastic but within my budget to boot. To this day I still adore, as do my many guests, the burnished, dramatic walls of my jewel box foyer in Manhattan. I layered on antique candle-burning sconces, a gilt mirror, and graphic and colorful abstract expressionist art, all to a grand effect. Over the years, the foyer walls have aged to a lovely patina, and they look even more wonderful today than they did the day I painted them.

OPPOSITE *Walls painted with silver radiator paint (and over-glazed with wide stripes), a poly-chromed Italian commode, and a gilt mirror all prove that you can indeed mix your metals.*

The Mural from My Childhood
LASTING IMPRESSIONS

When I was in the eighth grade, my parents decided to hire famed New Orleans–based muralist Elizabeth Hadden to hand paint the walls of our two-story foyer. My mother knew I would be fascinated with the artistry of the muralists, and she allowed me to stay home from school to watch and quietly study the craftsmen at work. I was entranced as they painted dramatic flora and fauna on all of the walls, both below and above the second-story gallery. Drawing inspiration from the beautiful Brunschwig & Fills silk fabric on my mother's Louis XVI settee, which depicted an Asian goddess surrounded by gardens, the artists literally transformed our entrance before my eyes. They created trees dripping with wisteria, water-colored iris, and other blossoms. Although it was not the taste of a teenager, I still appreciated how the artists created an entrance that completely personified my mother's exquisite femininity. For years, every time a guest entered our home they were transported to another world by the stunning and unique beauty of this work of art.

When embarking on writing this book, I wanted so much to include the painted foyer of my youth, but the house was sold nearly twenty years ago, and I feared that the murals would no longer be intact.

Thankfully, it turned out that the current owners had maintained the magnificent mural. They graciously invited me to visit and photograph the walls, and although I had not set foot in that room since college, once I walked into this dreamy foyer, I felt at home again. The magical walls were perfectly cared for over the years, thus proving such a beautiful investment can truly stand the test of time.

ABOVE AND OPPOSITE *The ethereal artistry on the foyer walls of my childhood home still lives on today.*

7

THE BELLE OF THE BALL

There's no denying it: every ball has a belle. And every room that I have really adored has that one magical object that dominates the room and captures everyone's imagination. Maybe it is an iconic piece of furniture or a sumptuous fabric. Whatever it is, you're in for the start of a wonderful, enduring affair. The belle will be the star of the show. Let everything else be the supporting characters.

BE PREPARED

You'll know when your love comes along, and, like a good Cub Scout or Brownie, when it does, it's always best to be prepared. You never know when or where you will discover that special must-have treasure that will help define your space. As you start your quest, keep your eyes and heart open—and a small notebook on hand. Document your favorite galleries or shops and record the measurements of your rooms, especially the wall spaces above existing furniture and around architectural elements. Depending on how far you are in your design process, keeping a few paint swatches as a helpful reminder of your palette is also a good idea. Even if you have the keenest eye for color and can match tones perfectly from memory, every bit of support helps. Just as a businessman would not be caught dead without his calling cards, while you are decorating or even thinking about your home (which, for me, is constantly), you should be armed with your swatches and notes at all times. There's no need to lug around an entire portfolio; your information can be as compact as a single, appropriate paint swatch with measurements jotted down on the back tucked away in your wallet.

However you decide to log the facts is up to you. Just make sure you're never out of town with your jaw hitting the floor in absolute, head-over-heels love with the perfect painting, and left questioning whether it will fit over the mantel. If you are, however, most galleries and some antiques shops will allow you to try paintings and furniture at home before purchasing. Others may give you time to think it over by offering you first refusal, so you'll have the first option to buy if someone else is interested.

Whether you actively search or just keep your eyes peeled, at one point or another it's bound to happen: your "belle of the ball" will ask you to dance. Say yes. The decisions we make based on love turn out to be much more lasting than those based on need. Think of these kinds of acquisitions as relationships that never fade or end. The best part is, just like a great friend, if they are treated well and with respect, they'll grow stronger and better with age.

OVERLEAF *This magnificent one-of-a-kind Chihuly glass sculpture is all that is needed in this living room. I believe that the fainting couch is simply there to catch swooning admirers.*

OPPOSITE *By placing a compelling portrait by Regina Loch Elvert in a less obvious area of the living room, the owners pulled together a smashing seating arrangement beneath their belle. The life-sized ceramic dog, from Neal auction, and the settee, covered in Kravet couture fabric, are inviting finishing touches.*

A CALL TO ARMOIRES

After landing my first Broadway show, I put a deposit down on an apartment, which was small but had great bones: high ceilings, decorative moldings, and gracious proportions. It had a foyer, maybe not two stories like my family home, but a four-by-six-foot space—enough for me to make my entrance and exit with my usual flair. I moved in my must-haves: a framed telegram from Helen Hayes welcoming me to Broadway and a poster of a Hans Hofmann painting, but as I contemplated my first steps in decorating my nest, I was somewhat overwhelmed. Fresh out of college, what did I really know about creating a home? All I knew was that I wanted one that I could make my own.

Then it came to me: my living room absolutely needed a tall, imposing French provincial armoire. Oh, yes, that is absolutely what would anchor my home and make it feel grounded. I was hell-bent on bringing the comfort and panache of New Orleans to New York by way of Magazine Street (by way of France). I called my friend Gay Wirth of Wirthmore Antiques and explained what I craved. I wasn't looking for something overly carved, or over the top, but rather something solid and weighty with a feeling of age and wisdom, characteristics that I did not possess at the time, but hoped I would one day.

Once I established my budget, Gay sent me a Polaroid of something she thought I might like. I gazed upon the beautiful lines of the perfect eighteenth-century walnut armoire, and I was hooked. There was something extremely sexy about the glossy French polish and tone of the rich wood. Gay shipped it to New York and it stood proudly in my living room, married to my apartment as if we had been together forever. I had made my first big-boy purchase, and although it was a bit daunting to write that check, I have never regretted it. Twenty years later, that gorgeous gal still reigns as the queen of the room.

ABOVE *It was love at first sight when I found my armoire.*

ABOVE *A custom-designed "tree bed" by metalsmith David Rockhold is all that's desired in this dreamy bedroom. The canopy of organic yet whimsical branches is serene when paired with Benjamin Moore Tea Light walls and antique Swedish demilunes.*

LEFT *A floor-to-ceiling scene-stealing nineteenth-century mirror, one of a pair, is actually original to the home. In the words of Dreamgirls' Effie White, it seems to sing, "and I'm telling you, I'm not going."*

ABOVE *A provocative work of art by harouni*
establishes the color direction for this dining room—
specifically, the tangerine silk curtains with detailed
olive green embroidery and citrus-hued striped fabric
on the chairs.

OPPOSITE *The girl can't help it. All eyes are drawn*
to the knockout yellow silk on this eighteenth-century
Louis XVI settee.

THE FAIREST PAINTING
OF THEM ALL

My dear mother always supported my career choice; in fact, she loved coming to New York to see me in every production I was part of, and I mean *every*. She was there whether it was a big Broadway blockbuster musical, or an off-off-Broadway experimental play performed in a church basement. And she more than supported Tom's and my decision to plant serious roots in New Orleans by purchasing a home—so much so that, if she could, she would have kicked her Ferragamo pumps high above her head in celebration. She kindly offered to give us a lovely and generous housewarming present to celebrate the event. The only stipulation was that it had to be something decorative that we would treasure forever. She wasn't thinking dishwasher or new gas stove. Frankly, neither was I.

Tom and I have always loved the whimsical yet weighty work of artist Blake Boyd, having admired his shows on more than one occasion. We were enthralled with his *Hard Luck Woman* series, which depicts Snow White being kissed by Prince Charming, and we instantly fell in love with *#13,* which is composed of black clay with gold, silver, and copper metallic leaf. As a beam of sunlight danced over the painting in the gallery, we found something very magical and romantic about it. We both knew that this work would be the perfect star of our living room, with its old-world charm and modern sensibility (thanks, Mom).

I adore our living room, which is on the second floor, nestled among the lush palms and oaks. The high vaulted ceilings and functioning French doors are innately romantic as sunlight streams in at all hours of the day.

We hung our new painting in a place of honor directly above the simply framed fireplace where light plays off the creamy walls and harlequin ivory and putty painted wood floors. Snow and her beau

---

I Think I Love You! As with everything in life, let your instincts guide you when picking your belle, and don't skimp. Even if you are just starting out, a standout item will raise the style quotient of the room, and, gradually, your aesthetic will develop. I'd rather have a week of gorgeous than a year of ugly, and as time progresses you will be happy with the decision to start with at least one high-end or well-designed piece.

Dealing with Dealers It is imperative to find and develop a relationship with a reputable and experienced antiques or art dealer who is mindful and respectful of your needs—and understands that you are not filling a museum, especially when you're first starting out. Frequent shops you like and ask questions about periods and styles, and learn from the curators of the individual stores. Just like making a friend, you'll know when you both click and when a trust is born. Although it's customary to discuss the "best" price, keep in mind that this is a business. Your dealer will keep you abreast of new shipments and possible sales or markdowns. If there is a specific item you are searching for, make sure your dealer knows, no matter how obscure it is. They might find it halfway around the world and can easily ship it to you. Be wary of anyone trying to pressure you into a quick deal. Most dealers who are worth their salt love what they are doing with a fervent passion, and will treat you with equal attention and care if you are eyeing a piece that costs five hundred dollars or five thousand.

are breathtaking from sunrise to sunset. We left the windows bare, unfettered by fussy window treatments, so the panoramic vistas of treetops and church steeples are visible at all times. The beautiful metallic tones gleam as they are kissed by light, and we took this as our cue for the rest of the room's decoration.

In keeping with the clean lines of the painting, we kept the furniture plan spare. A pair of 1940s armchairs from Jon Vaccari Design, in natural linen, flank the fireplace, and a contemporary glass and metal coffee table allows a continuation of light.

We chose the room's accessories carefully to incorporate and mirror the marvelous luster within the painting. I love the pair of gold coin pillows, the silver porcelain coral vase, and the burnished gold mosaic box in glass, which are all from Hazelnut. These choices are a perfect juxtaposition to the aged metallic on my grandfather's carved German court jester and a pair of antique crusty gilt Venetian lanterns found in the Paris flea market. It is all a perfect marriage, which occurs often in design as in life: something or someone special opens the door, and all we have to do is follow their generous lead. Just like old Snow White, I hope to live happily ever after in this light-filled tree house.

OPPOSITE *I reupholstered my grandmother's wing chair in a mushroom-colored cut-velvet fabric with a leaf motif as a subtle nod to the great outdoors. The Raku bowl that Tom gave me for my birthday is from Shadyside Pottery and all of the metallic shades we love are richly captured in it's intricate glaze.*

LOVE FOUND A WAY

Karla Katz is a friend, great designer, and owner of one of the most intriguing antiques shops on Magazine Street. She makes frequent trips to Paris and the south of France for her design clients and to stock her fabulous store. Her eye for decorative antiques is unparalleled in the business, and I check out her wares several times a month just for inspiration (sometimes I want to bring in a cot to live among Karla's great discoveries). During one of her trips to Paris, Karla fell in love with a French trumeau mirror that she found while visiting her favorite dealers on the Left Bank. The eighteenth-century gilt piece had so much character, so much patina, with layers and layers of chalky paint and hints of gold leaf—and it was ten feet tall! The proportions were outstanding and everything about it screamed to Karla, "Take me with you." Karla knew it was best to follow her instinct; however, the mirror's height raised a perplexing issue. No home that she knew of could possibly accommodate such a grand trumeau, which is traditionally placed above a commode or mantel. One this tall would require a fourteen- to sixteen-foot ceiling—and those don't grow on trees. Karla followed her heart and bought the piece not really knowing what she would do with it, but she had a gut feeling that something great could be done with this belle. So with her imagination and inspired vision, she gave the trumeau a whole new life, function, and purpose. Giovanni Bonomo, a master craftsman and antiques restorer, removed the mirror at the bottom of the piece and lovingly redesigned it to house a wonderful working fireplace in her own home. Needless to say, Karla's trumeau and fireplace became the showstopper and a warm, vibrant centerpiece in her charming, dramatic living room. Far and away, this is one of my favorite examples of repurposing beautiful architectural antiques. A trumeau that might have spent years sitting alone in a warehouse has crossed the ocean, landed in New Orleans, and is a source of constant warmth in its reincarnation.

TIP **I cannot stress enough that if you love it, get it. Like Karla, you may have to use some extra brain power or imagination to work it all out, but never let something you love slip away. In my book, regret is a four-letter word.**

OPPOSITE *A contemporary biomorphic glass sculpture by Carlos Zervigon found at Cole Pratt Gallery lives happily among Karla's many antiques—a Biedermeier chair covered in vintage Scalamandré leopard velvet and a French crystal chandelier from the 1920s.*

A Work of Art
ALL IN THE FAMILY ROOM

Tripp Friedler, like many people with a great eye for art, had been admiring the artist Elemore Morgan Jr.'s colorful and evocative works for years, hoping to add one soon to his vast art collection. Meanwhile, his wife, Heidi, was embarking on the redecoration of their family room and needed a dramatic anchor. The space, a blank canvas, was quite big, and one main wall was absolutely begging for a colorful, large-scale work of art to lead the way to a fabulous design scheme for the rest of the room. When they walked into a showing of the artist's newest paintings, they were floored by one landscape in particular. Layers of fiery pinks and verdant green pigment explode off of the forty-three by eighty-eight-inch canvas, which glows with exuberance. They both knew they had found the *one*.

Once the painting was hung, the emotional and visual heartbeat of the room emerged, and the design plan was off and running. The piece initiated the bright color palette: several shades of fresh, lush greens, vibrant tangerine, vivid hot pink, all bursting with the same life and energy of the canvas and employed cheerfully throughout the room. Heidi had fabric custom colored and printed in lime and grass green for window treatments to establish a green backdrop for the room. She then layered saturated leaf and citron hues in stripes and geometric patterns on the upholstery and pillows with the occasional hit of hot pink in lacquered boxes and textiles. This significant design statement, a virtual garden of green, is as abundant and lively as the subject matter in the painting.

Additional punches of accent color, also derived from the painting, come into play next. I love the fuchsia-lacquered ceramic lamps, and the oversized celery green painted coffee table, large enough for board games and snacks in front of the TV. Heidi repaints the coffee table every year to hide the inevitable wear-and-tear that results from its use in this family room. Everything in the room seems to say a big cheerful "hello" to the painting. Other art in the room echoes this tight color story and reverberates with livliness just like the overall mood of the room.

OPPOSITE *An Ida Kohlmeyer Abstract Expressionist painting, a vintage chair and ottoman, and an adorable homespun embroidered pillow are dutiful supporting characters to the belle of the room (pictured on page 179).*

ABOVE *Custom-colored screen-printed linen drapes from Raoul Textiles, a John Alexander oil, and a cheerful game table from Pottery Barn all live within the palette defined by the main attraction.*

RIGHT *The wall-to-wall work of art that the Friedlers fell in love with jibes perfectly with the engaging personality of the lady of the house.*

8

MAKE YOUR OWN KIND OF MUSIC

I learned long ago that in order to be a good actor, you must be fearless, keep yourself open to new experiences, and allow yourself to fail (several times) in the process. Only then will you learn to trust your instincts and be confident that your individuality is your greatest strength. With design, move to your own groove, dance to your own beat, and bend a trend or two along the way. Throw out the rules and step outside of the box and your decoration decisions will follow effortlessly.

FEAR NOT

Whenever I need a boost of confidence or validation to try something new, I crank up The Mamas & The Papas' hit "Make Your Own Kind of Music" and listen to Mama Cass belting out the sage advice to do my own thing and not worry about what others think. My mother imparted this same philosophy to me; she always said that sometimes life can feel like a race, but just like the racehorses, you have to put your blinders on and run at your own speed, and never compare yourself to others. Putting other people's opinions ahead of your own is the surest way to zap your creativity and reduce your decorating mojo to a design formula. Use someone else's game plan and you'll only get predictable results that are void of the most important design element: *you.* Leave the formulas to the chemists.

One factor that often cripples the design process is the fear of making mistakes or getting it wrong. Well, guess what? You are going to make mistakes, and things may not work out as planned—that's life. But never make a decision based on fear; one can never be truly stylish without taking a risk or two.

OH, THE PLACES YOU'LL GO

Expose yourself to every aspect of design and look for it in all the right places. Frequent art museums and galleries as much as possible, and don't overlook exhibits that dare to shake things up a bit. Take a closer look at the architecture in your own town and in all the places you visit. It is amazing how different cities have such different footprints. Don't overlook details on dwellings like shutter colors, awning stripes, and even window boxes, as they often are a clear indication of the neighborhood's inherent style. Make travel a priority, especially trips to exotic places, which opens doors to design ideas that we never dreamed possible. There are a multitude of décor elements and concepts you can incorporate

TIP Discovering what makes you most happy is the essential key to designing your home. If you can achieve that, the rest will fall into place. An actor's trick I discovered long ago can be applied. Once you are fully immersed in your character and he is under your skin, it is virtually impossible to make a false move.

OVERLEAF *Having grown up in a family playground of roller coasters and amusement park rides, I fell in love with this antique Irish carousel horse that I placed beneath my staircase as a fond reminder of my youth.*

CLOCKWISE FROM TOP LEFT *Whimsical touches that tickle my fancy: a faience lamb from Normandy breaks away from the flock as a dining room center-piece, while a leopard's spots change atop formal silk drapes. Fun inside a bubble is not just for Glinda the good witch, it also belongs in the bedroom. I love talking shop about feathering nests with artist Kaki Foley.*

from your travels—think of the rich color palates of India and the south of France or the intricate tribal textiles of Africa. Every time my parents returned from a long trip, something special was bound to show up on our doorstep not long after. Though furniture and large pieces can be difficult to ship back from abroad, smaller pieces can be easily carried home. On a trip to visit friends in Tokyo, Tom and I carried back, literally on our backs, twelve place settings of Japanese earthenware, and from Paris, we bought gorgeous iron cookware and Baccarat highball glasses of a pattern not available in the United States. Everywhere you go, whether it's abroad or here at home, keep your eyes and heart open to different design influences.

When I first arrived in the Big Apple, I loved to get lost in New York. I would jump on a subway and randomly ride to a distant stop that I'd never seen, then explore the buildings and styles as I found my way home. Even today I still seek out different neighborhoods in my own hometown and study the varied architectural designs and colors at play.

Recently, I arrived early to an appointment in a neighborhood of New Orleans that I was completely unfamiliar with. Although I had driven along Esplanade Avenue near Bayou St. John and dined at some of the area restaurants, I had never really ventured off onto the side streets. With fifteen minutes to kill, I meandered and discovered some of the most unique and beautiful examples of nineteenth- and early twentieth–century architecture, in a variety of styles that I'd never seen before, even though they had always been right under my nose. Being able to pull back, notice, and appreciate great design is the secret to zeroing in on what makes your heart sing. Bringing those passions into your home helps you establish feeling and mood, and defines your spaces with your own unique signature.

MAKE ME SMILE

Move confidently in your own direction, but remember that the path is not necessarily straight and narrow; it can be winding and wide. Be open to switching gears, finding different solutions, and being original. You can color outside of the lines and you can have a tremendous amount of fun if you are flexible, creative, and maintain your sense of humor. Sometimes

TIP Above all, what I love most is to be a tourist in my own town or to take a closer look at what is in my own backyard. A trip to Italy or Bali is definitely exhilarating, and a day at the beach staring at the ocean and collecting shells is always inspiring. But your own city can be a source of great discovery, too. Feed your artistic side by seeing plays, listening to live music, learning how to tango, or taking a drawing class. Great design is everywhere and inspiration abounds.

the most rewarding solution is as simple as a witty and clever twist on a very basic idea. Years ago, I wanted to create an old-new mix in my living room by flanking a very contemporary painting with a pair of antique bronze gilt sconces. I searched high and low for months, my heart set on the idea, but everything I found was either entirely the wrong scale or way beyond my budget. Just as I was about to give up on finding my dream sconces, I happened to be in Jane Stubbs's boutique (she now shows her collections at Bergdorf Goodman) for a sale she was having on some of her fantastic prints and original drawings. And lo and behold, there they were: hand-engraved *renderings* of empire sconces. I had those babies slipped into gilt frames, and voila, my "sconces" were hanging on my walls. To tell the truth, I like them better than if I had the real deal: much less dusting. So be open, be clever, have fun, and toss out convention if it makes you happy!

Discover what really makes you smile, and once you've found it, take it one step further. The spaces I've showcased in this chapter are great examples of how the owners followed their passions. To me, they are "living the dream": their rooms are all stunning examples of their signature style and exemplify what it truly means to make your own kind of music, all in your own home.

ABOVE *I am taking it as a compliment, but I've been told my grandfather was thinking of me when he brought this theatrical carved jester back from Germany. It now sits proudly on my coffee table, lending plenty of whimsy to my living room.*

An Art Deco Dream

I GET A KICK OUT OF YOU

My dear friends Joe Keenan and Gerry Bernardi's home, Wiseacres, is one of my favorite places in California. Although it sits atop the hills of Los Angeles, at first glance, the rapturous grounds and main structure's stone and whitewashed wooden exterior resemble a picture postcard of a classic Connecticut or upstate New York grand ranch home. The winding flagstone steps leading to the front door are surrounded by exquisitely tended beds of foliage, with impressive abundance of white rose bushes and blooming annuals. Once inside, though, it's as if you've stepped into a Hollywood dream: everything about Joe and Gerry's clean, bright, and streamlined deco home seems to suggest that at any moment, Fred Astaire or Carole Lombard might make an entrance and join in the festivities.

At Joe and Gerry's annual Derby Day party, I was pleased to meet D. Crosby Ross, the famed designer who worked on the interior design of their home. As we all chatted, I learned of the renovation and of Gerry's and especially Joe's affinity for the deco period. They both adore the elegant sophistication of the era. Joe is an avid collector of autographed first-editions of works by Cole Porter, and Gerry adores the classic lines of deco furniture as well as the definitive accessories, especially clocks, from that glamorous time. When they began their collaboration, Gerry and Joe jokingly remember wanting the home to be "Tallulah Bankhead in Connecticut." By this they meant chic urban interiors with a clean deco-meets-modern feel to reflect their New York sensibilities, while also celebrating the indoor/outdoor lifestyle that is quintessentially Southern California. Keeping this vision in mind, they filled their perfectly appointed home with a collection of priceless furniture, decorations, and art, all arranged so beautifully that it never feels like a stage, but rather like a home that allows Joe and Gerry to live stylishly and to generously entertain.

At the drop of a hat (perhaps a silk top hat), Gerry can whip up a fabulous dinner for six, and whether it's a gourmet feast or designer hamburgers, he always serves his meals elegantly using the finest china, silver, and crystal. I completely agree with their philosophy of enjoying their beautiful collections as they were meant to be, rather than keeping them behind glass or under lock and key. Like Auntie Mame said, "Live, live, live!"

The entrance gallery hosts a fabulous French art deco burled walnut credenza with a black marble inset top. Gerry keeps a mudroom—or what some would call a

florist shop—downstairs. There, he creates lush, dazzling floral arrangements. Atop the credenza are two of his creations, the Casablanca lilies in the Pauline vase by Baccarat and the roses in a vase by Daum, and their presence is graced by one of the many clocks in Gerry's collection. This 1920s example, made of nickel by Mappin & Webb, sits next to a polished nickel cigarette box by James Mont. The pièce de résistance is the portrait that is believed to be that of Tallulah herself. The artist, Etienne Ret, moved to Hollywood in 1934 and was known for painting celebrities of the period; for the owners, this painting was a must-have, and now she reigns at the center of the entire home.

In the informal dining and screening room, on the paneled far wall, is an accordion fold Pommele Sapele fireplace mantel with polished Rosso Verona marble. The room just evolves perfectly from there. Crosby designed the palm tree–inspired fire screen, based on a photograph of doors to a Parisian town house. In front is a pair of ebonized caramel leather steamer chairs, and serving as a coffee table is an American empire low table, which features more of Gerry's collection of exquisite accessories.

The seating area sits on a "baby tiger" print leather hide rug and sisal. In the windowed bay looking out onto the gracious patio is a breathtaking Austrian

OVERLEAF *Bronze silk upholstered walls are a sublime setting for this sensual vignette in my friend's formal living room.*

ABOVE *An oil portrait of the notorious Tallulah Bankhead is simply divine, dahling.*

OPPOSITE *This charming and masculine room looks out onto lavish gardens complete with koi ponds and flowering bougainvillea.*

Biedermeier round breakfast table with nineteenth-century Russian Gothic side chairs. For a touch of whimsy, Gerry added a black plaster bust of society impresario Earl Blackwell and a card reading "To the best-dressed man."

A charming vignette consists of the 1929 French art deco secretary made of Macassar ebony and pergament by Dominique. Above it hangs a gorgeous Christian Vincent painting. The sensuous masked siren was the logo for the very first Les Girls breast cancer research fundraiser and signifies an annual event that Gerry helped create. Christian generously donated the painting to the silent auction, and after a bidding war, Joe and Gerry took home the wonderful painting, which has immeasurable heartfelt meaning.

I have loved every visit, every party, every dinner, and every moment in this elegant home, and it is the perfect reflection of its delightful owners.

An Artist's Home
BIRDS OF A FEATHER

Gretchen Weller Howard and I attended the same high school, and even then I knew she traveled to her own artistic beat. Besides being one of the most attractive girls at Isidore Newman School, she was clearly one of the most gifted. Her paintings and sculptures graced the hallowed halls, and, if I recall correctly, usually with blue ribbons attached. Gretchen comes from a family of artists, so it was only natural that she knows exactly what to do with a paintbrush. Besides excelling as an artist whose works are shown through the exclusive Søren Christensen gallery, she is also a sought-after decorative painter. She paints distinctive finishes, patterns, and designs on walls, floors, furnishings, and even fabrics. Above all, she has one of the most creative and inspiring spirits I know, and she shares her love for all things beautiful with her family and friends.

In her home—a hundred-year-old raised side hall cottage that she shares with her husband, Peter, and two daughters— Gretchen has created a true artist's space that celebrates her passion for art and family. For Gretchen, art should not be exclusively highbrow, for museum walls only. Instead, art is an active pursuit in her home and plays a major role in how the entire decoration comes together. Upon opening

her vibrant purple front door, which lets you know something unique is to follow, I'm completely knocked out by her foyer. The small vestibule features a striking wallpaper in the most luscious shade of violet and substantial woodwork moldings that she painted to complement the saturated hue. Above a nineteenth-century maple chest hangs a whimsical, oversized modern sculpture of a nest. It was created from reclaimed branches covered with decoupage newspaper and sheet music. Gretchen loves this piece for many reasons; not only is it charming, but it was also created by her close friend and fellow artist Kaki Foley. But what really speaks to her is the symbolism of the nest: since the house is raised and the living quarters are on the second floor high up in the trees, she feels it's most appropriate that guests are greeted with this representation of the cozy home she has created within.

The living room and dining room are blanketed in more art. Light streams in from the bank of windows at the rear of the house, making the entire space glow. The stunning focus of the room is one of Gretchen's paintings, a large-scale mixed-media work featuring a multitude of her signature birds in lavenders, turquoise, and rosy pink. The piece, called *Seeking Truth in Beauty,* reigns supreme in the room at this

moment and lives atop a slate and gold leaf iron console flanked by a pair of deco mirrored urns made into lamps. Gretchen used violet fabric paint to decorate a pony-hair ottoman with a Greek key design that she can slide out as needed for extra seating. She hand-poured a ceramic vase for flowers. The rest of the living room is filled with furniture inherited from family members and lots and lots of additional canvases.

Gretchen is always moving her art— even during my last visit, she was rearranging pieces. She believes all her art works together no matter where it hangs, because it is an organic extension of her personal style (just as one might not buy whole outfits but pieces that can mix and match). I love this idea and marveled as she put this painting there and moved that painting here, without moving a single hook or nail.

The light- and art-filled hallway is by far the happiest hall I have ever seen. Gretchen has hung portraits, landscapes, and abstracts, starting in the center of the hall, with a plan to completely cover the walls over time. Most of the paintings are her works; many are her father's, the noted artist Dell Weller; two are by her mother; and there is even one by a budding artist, her young daughter. Confidently following her own passionate intuition, Gretchen has created a remarkable display that fully represents her love for her art and family.

OVERLEAF *A handmade wallpaper from SJW Studios provides a strong dose of potent color, giving a small entranceway immediate drama.*

ABOVE *A joyous infusion of sundrenched pigments—coral, cerulean, jade, and persimmon— take flight on this oversized canvas.*

OPPOSITE *Gretchen hand-stenciled her gray-washed wood floors with gold leaf and punctuated the hall doors with the same daring hue as the foyer, Benjamin Moore's Central Mauve.*

An Eighteenth-Century French Kitchen
AMOUR AT FIRST SIGHT

Sometimes things are just meant to be. Several times each year, Lucy Mitchell frequented Magazine Street when she visited New Orleans from her home in Texas for dining, shopping, and inspiration. Wirthmore Antiques was a must-see on her list of fabulous stops, and a visit to Gay Wirth's magical shop—filled with drop-dead gorgeous collectibles— always made Lucy's heart sing. When she started to think about creating a dream house on her farm in Texas, which would be built from and filled with all things European, she of course turned to Gay for brainstorming and design consultation. Lucy and Gay share a deep passion for restoring and salvaging architectural pieces, and Lucy's true love is recycling antique architectural findings into a new construction. She wanted every beam, window, and door to be authentic, aged, and brimming with the soul and patina that only antiques can bring to a design project. And she was willing to wait while some serious hunting and collecting went on to find just the right bits and pieces to fuel the project. And then "it" happened.

While on a buying trip in France, Gay came upon an entire building for sale in the village of Précy-sous-Thil in the Côte d'Or region. What fascinated her was the interior, complete with an original spice shop still intact and glowing with enchanting warm honey-colored wood, original paint, and aged glass. Walls and walls were lined with glass doors and display shelves, charming drawers of all sizes, and beautiful hardware. As is often the case in these situations, the proprietor was not Internet savvy, and all he could offer Gay to forward on to Lucy were old-fashioned Polaroid pictures. And so as Lucy pored over the dark, unfocused images, she fell in love long distance and her kitchen was born. With a huge leap of faith, Lucy bought the entire spice shop. Sometimes you have to go to great lengths for love, and as the spice shop made its way across the ocean, the design project took flight.

Lucy ultimately made the decision to maintain her farm in Texas but to construct the dream house in New Orleans. So her renovation, with the spice shop as the anchor, actually resides in a two-thousand-square-foot midrise condo on St. Charles Avenue. To walk into Lucy's home is to walk into another world. Every detail has been lovingly attended to, and the marriage of the antique windows, doors, fittings, and materials to modern-day design and function is stunning. The craftsmanship is outstanding: eighteenth-century French ocher and terra-cotta tile from Marseille create a rustic floor in the dining room; the kitchen ceiling of Provençal wood beams and plaster is one of the prettiest I have ever seen; and the walls throughout the home are hand plastered with a modern product called American Clay, which oozes with texture and romance. In the kitchen, I love the French antique zinc shop counter that was custom-designed in Provence and fitted as an island for the stove and cabinetry. The marvelous collection of French pottery and rare, eighteenth-century faience platters fill the cabinet beautifully. But it is the smallest of gestures that truly makes me smile: iconic antique Provençal fabric for a valance in the kitchen and a faience lamb from Normandy peeking around an antique covered tureen on the dining room table. Just a step or two from the streetcar on St. Charles Avenue, and you are in the south of France. And there is no mistaking that Lucy is living her dream.

OVERLEAF *A romantic oil painting of a port in St. Tropez by noted French artist Guillaume Roger hangs above a handsome eighteenth-century applewood buffet from the south of France.*

RIGHT *To create a window where none existed, a pair of antique demilune transoms were turned on their sides and joined in the middle, allowing for a "spectacular view" of an Elemore Morgan Jr., painting and Milton Hebald sculpture.*

My Mardi Gras Mambo
BEFORE THE PARADE PASSES BY

I have wildly celebrated Mardi Gras since I was a baby. From my very first carnival to my senior year at Tulane, I never missed one Fat Tuesday family celebration on St. Charles Avenue. Every aspect of New Orleans history and its pageantry has always fascinated me. I am completely enraptured by the detailed ornamentation and opulently designed floats that promenade under the canopies of majestic oaks dripping with Spanish moss. The dancing torchlights, carried by the flambeaux carriers, always create a mesmerizing visual effect. Some people come to hear the bands, some love to catch the beads and trinkets, but I love to stand back and take in the beauty of the float art. Mardi Gras is the greatest free show on earth and a feast for all the senses, but especially the visual. (Interestingly enough, the organization for Rex, the king of Mardi Gras, is actually called School of Design.)

Our carriage house in New Orleans was connected to the property of a St. Charles Avenue mansion where all the Mardi Gras parades pass. Needless to say, our home became a carnival hub during the festivities. That first year back home, I realized that I had not witnessed one of these beloved extravaganzas of my youth in more than ten years. I had forgotten how vibrant, and fun the gold leaf–tipped papier-mâché float art truly is.

As much as I love to watch a parade, I've also had the great pleasure of riding in a few. And as thrilling as that is, I always felt that living with one would be heaven. Since once a year was not enough for me, I had an idea to bring this magic into our home. I envisioned a display similar to the way people collect and display other great American folk art. I called up the captain of a carnival krewe, a friend of mine, who gave me a tour of the den and floats. He let me choose a pair of majestic blooms that I displayed on our dining room wall. Tom artistically arranged the flowers on the wall, where they were long the topic of conversation. Everyone smiled when they saw the float art—children thought it was cool, adults reveled in the whimsy—but the main effect was that it just made us happy. It was a risky choice to display gigantic tempera-painted papier-mâché flowers with a crystal chandelier and seventeenth-century lanterns, but I'm the bouncer at this club, and they made the cut.

OPPOSITE *In order to let my Mardi Gras float decorations shine, I lacquered the walls in Benjamin Moore Chocolate Sundae and used my unfussy toile in Café au Lait for the drapes. But these wild wall hangings still didn't stop me from installing a beaded crystal chandelier sold through Hazelnut (hey, who says you have to choose your drama?).*

RESOURCES

HOME FURNISHINGS AND ACCESSORIES

Bergdorf Goodman
754 Fifth Avenue
New York, New York
212-753-7300
www.bergdorfgoodman.com

Hazelnut
5515 Magazine Street
New Orleans, Louisiana 70115
504-891-2424
www.hazelnutneworleans.com

Lūm Vintage Lighting
3806 Magazine Street
New Orleans, Louisiana 70115
504-939-1474
www.shoplum.com

Nola Rugs
3944 Magazine Street
New Orleans, Louisiana 70115
504-891-3304
www.nolarugs.com

Perch
2844 Magazine Street
New Orleans, Louisiana 70115
504-899-2122
www.perch-home.com

ANTIQUES

Balzac Antiques
3506 Magazine Street
New Orleans, Louisiana 70115
504-899-2668
www.balzacantiques.com

Blackman Cruz
836 North Highland Avenue
Los Angeles, California 90038
323-466-8600
www.blackmancruz.com

Jon Vaccari Design
1912 St. Charles Avenue
New Orleans, Louisiana 70130
504-899-7632
www.jonvaccaridesign.com

Karla Katz and Co.
4017 Magazine Street
New Orleans, Louisiana 70115
504-897-0061
karlakatz@aol.com

Keil's Antiques
325 Royal Street
New Orleans, Louisiana 70130
504-522-4552
www.keilsantiques.com

Moss Antiques
411 Royal Street
New Orleans, Louisiana 70130
504-522-3981
www.mossantiques.com

Royal Antiques
309 Royal Street
New Orleans, Louisiana 70130
504-524-7033
www.royalantiques.com

Wirthmore Antiques
3727 Magazine Street
New Orleans, Louisiana 70115
504-269-0660
www.wirthmoreantiques.com

ART GALLERIES AND ARTISTS

Arthur Roger Gallery
432 and 434 Julia Street
New Orleans, Louisiana 70130
504-522-1999
www.arthurrogergallery.com

Art Student Showcase
248 Lafayette Street
New York, New York 10012
212-941-9471

Bryan Burkey
bryan.burkey@gmail.com

Cole Pratt Gallery
3800 Magazine Street
New Orleans, Louisiana 70115
504-891-6789
www.coleprattgallery.com

Gretchen Howard
gretchenwhoward@yahoo.com

Kaki Foley
www.tatterdesign.com

CLOCKWISE FROM TOP LEFT *My favorite wares at Hazelnut: A gold-leafed handmade work of art from my Gulf Coast wildlife series of reverse decoupage glass platters features the majestic winter egret; scalloped placemats, hand-sewn napkins, and charming coasters in Delphine New Orleans Toile are elegant accessories for any table setting; gleaming lead crystal decanters and masculine double old fashioned barware embellished with fourteen-karat gold Greek key epitomize glam to me; a Magnolia New Orleans Toile lacquered ottoman tray is the ideal addition to any bar or living room.*

Mario Villa
504-523-8731
www.mariovilla.net

Nahan Fine Art
540 Royal Street
New Orleans, Louisiana 70130
504-913-8877
www.nohanfineart.com

Shelley Venema
559-738-8657
www.laurelwilder.com

Sonia O'Mara Stuebe
32 Union Square East, #1017
New York, New York 10003
www.soniaomara.com

AUCTION HOUSES

Bonhams & Butterfields
7601 Sunset Boulevard
Los Angeles, California 90046
323-850-7500
www.bonhams.com

Doyle New York
175 East Eighty-seventh Street
New York, New York 10128
212-427-2730
www.DoyleNewYork.com

Neal Auction Company
4038 Magazine Street
New Orleans, Louisiana 70115
504-899-5329
www.nealauction.com

New Orleans Auction
801 Magazine Street
New Orleans, Louisiana 70130
800-501-0277
504-566-1849
www.neworleansauction.com

DESIGN SERVICES

Chrestia, Staub, Pierce
7219 Perrier Street
New Orleans, Louisiana 70118
504-866-6677
www.cspdesign.com

Decoration & Design Building
979 Third Avenue
New York, New York 10022
212-759-5408
www.ddbuilding.com

Heidi Friedler Interiors
hhfriedler@aol.com

Interior Design Building
306 East Sixty-first Street
New York, New York 10021
212-833-7042

Melissa Rufty
MMR Interiors
3806 Magazine Street
Suite One
New Orleans, Louisiana 70115
504-899-7020
www.mmrinteriors.com

Suzie Allain Interiors
www.suzieallain.com

Williamson Designs/La Vieille Maison
3646 Magazine Street
New Orleans, Louisiana 70115
504-899-4945
www.williamsondesigns.net

FABRICS AND TRIMS

Delk & Morrison Inc.
1010 Conti Street
New Orleans, Louisiana 70112
504-529-4939

Interior Fabrics
3200 Severn Avenue, #112
Metairie, Louisiana 70002
504-454-8164
www.fabricresource.com

M & J Trimming
1008 Sixth Avenue
New York, New York 10018
www.mjtrim.com

Promenade Fine Fabrics
1520 St. Charles Avenue
New Orleans, Louisiana 70130
504-522-1488

Tinsel Trading Company
1 West Thirty-seventh Street
New York, New York 10018
212-730-1030
www.tinseltrading.com

ARTISANS AND RESTORERS

Aguilar's Upholstery
8730 Oak Street
New Orleans, Louisiana 70118
504-866-3171
Furniture upholstery

Elizabeth II Lighting
3951 Magazine Street
New Orleans, Louisiana 70115
504-895-5314
Lamp restoration (will also rewire found objects into lamps)

Mike Hull
504-259-8043
Installation services such as drapery and wall upholstery

Giovanni Bonomo
The Renaissance Shop
2104 Magazine Street
New Orleans, Louisiana 70130
504-525-8568
Furniture Restoration

ACKNOWLEDGMENTS

MY IMMEDIATE REACTION when approached by my lovely editor, Angelin Borsics, to create a design book was that same unbridled exuberance I felt when cast in my first Broadway show. Design and decoration has enthralled me my entire life, and I couldn't wait to share my passion, ideas, and philosophies. Little did I realize how tricky and sometimes daunting this endeavor would prove as I was already penning my first book, *She Ain't Heavy, She's My Mother* (my "momoir"). But with our shared New Orleans roots, Angelin was the ideal guide through these uncharted and sometimes murky waters. Thank you to my agent, Eric Meyers, and my entire Clarkson Potter family, especially my book designer, Stephanie Huntwork. Working with master photographer Kerri McCaffety was a dream. Her brilliant work illuminated the inherent beauty and individuality of every space, causing me to fall in love with room after room, shot after shot. If not for the courage of this fearless crew, this minnow would have been lost.

Writers and editors in the design world have enthusiastically supported Hazelnut from the very beginning, and I am eternally grateful to them all, especially Deb Shriver, Stephen Drucker, Newell Turner, Orli Ben D'Or, Suzanne Zuckerman, Rene Peck, Susan Langenhennig, Marianne Rohrlich, and Joyce Wadler. This actor/designer appreciates the unique relationship between an audience and the stage, and, as such, our Hazelnut customers are a constant source of inspiration; they keep me on my toes and propel my creativity.

I am wild about styling and accessorizing rooms. Thankfully, my talented design team, Katy Danos and Tom Cianfichi, indulged this passion. They often did the work of six or seven people and were never afraid to roll up their sleeves and join me in getting a little dirty, in order to make every shot fabulous. Our three-musketeer camaraderie saw us through many challenging days, nights, and tight deadlines. After endless hours of back-to-back shoots in these gorgeous trenches, we still enjoyed each other's company over some well-deserved QTW (quittin' time wine).

Finally, I must say that this book happened because of one person: Katy. Every project could benefit enormously from her great wit, writing talent, stamina, and whip cracking. Her knowledge and zeal for design is unrivaled, and it was immeasurably helpful to volley ideas with someone whose taste and judgment I trust implicitly. What a comfort and joy to have such a safety net throughout this writing process.

To all of my readers, I invite you to wend your way down to New Orleans, visit us at Hazelnut, and celebrate living in big, easy style.

CREDITS

My heartfelt thanks go to the many interior designers and artisans who generously shared their talent and craft. Showcasing their homes, their work for clients, and their beautiful shops was an honor, and I celebrate their creativity with immense respect and admiration. The Big Easy has no shortage of spirit, style, and soul, and I could have easily tripled the amount of pages in this book with stunning images of home after home.

Suzie Allain, 18, 58, 80, 118, 148, 149, 150, 151; Gerrie Bremermann, 38, 85; Chrestia, Staub, Pierce, 39, 135, 160; John Chrestia, 127; Katy Danos, 15, 56; Tom Delcambre, 25 (top right); John Edgar, 25 (top left); Kaki Foley, 53, 143, 183 (bottom left); Heidi Friedler, 55, 76, 77, 78, 79, 88, 91, 125, 132, 177, 178, 179, 183 (bottom right); Valorie Hart, 65, 145; Gretchen Weller Howard, 26 (bottom left), 190, 192, 193; Karla Katz, 52, 66, 75, 82, 93 (top left), 103, 121, 129, 153, 174; Ann Koerner, 164; Beth Kohnke, 2, 22; Renee Lejeune, 63, 68; Ned Marshall, 5, 14, 54, 70, 86, 157; LM Pagano, 12; Peter Patout, 134; Karyl Pierce Paxton, 124, 168; Renee Picotte, 25 (bottom right); Caroline Robert, 36, 93 (bottom right), 105, 109, 110, 111, 138, 163, 166, 167; Melissa Rufty, front cover, 16, 17, 21, 33, 34, 35, 60, 71, 72, 93 (top right), 94, 95, 101, 102, 104, 113, 114, 117, 123, 128, 137, 140, 146, 147, 152; D. Crosby Ross, 93 (bottom left), 186, 188, 189; Babs Watkins and Nelta Culver, 26 (top left); Tanga Winstead, 122; Gay Wirth and Lucy Mitchell, 26 (bottom right), 74, 183 (top left), 194, 197.

Thank you to the following homeowners who welcomed us with warm hospitality and made us feel like honored guests rather than the intruders we often were as we photographed their spaces and shared their stories.

Andrée and Jay Batt; Joe Keenan and Gerry Bernardi; Lauren and George Brower; Leslie and Bryan Burkey; Sean Cummings; Sally and Richard Edrington; Jennifer and Fred Heebe; Elly and Merritt Lane; Lucy Mitchell; Melissa and Bill Myers; Lauré and David Pons, Vincent Saia and Glynn Stephens; Bridget and Ronnie Vinson.

INDEX

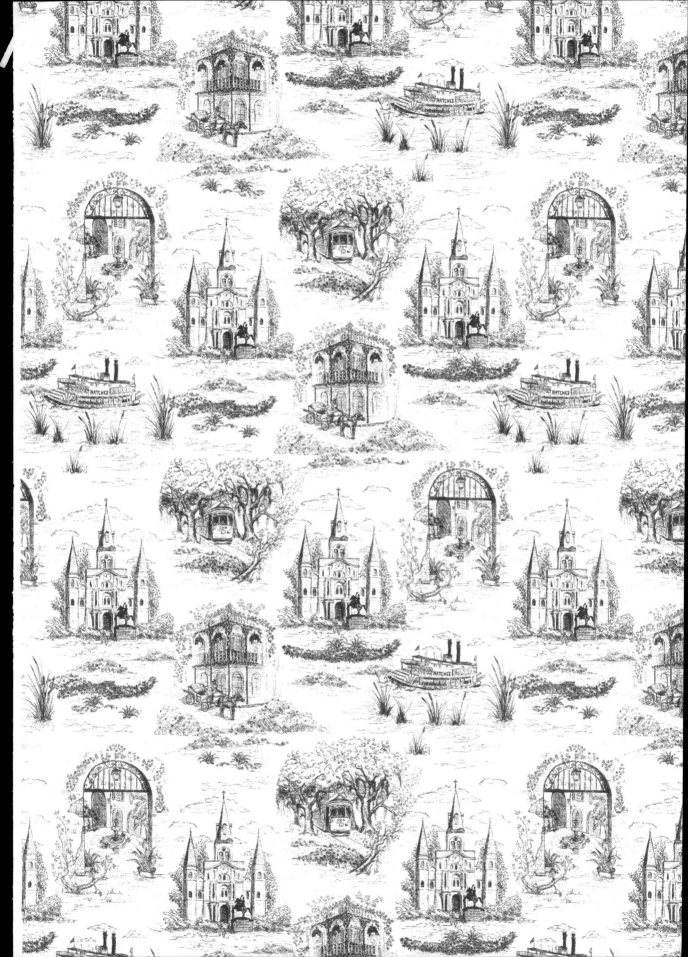